Edwin P. Parker

Sunday-School Songs

a new collection of hymns and tunes specially prepared for the use of Sunday-schools and for social and family worship. Third Edition

Edwin P. Parker

Sunday-School Songs
a new collection of hymns and tunes specially prepared for the use of Sunday-schools and for social and family worship. Third Edition

ISBN/EAN: 9783337265939

Printed in Europe, USA, Canada, Australia, Japan

Cover: Foto ©Lupo / pixelio.de

More available books at **www.hansebooks.com**

SUNDAY-SCHOOL SONGS

A New Collection of Hymns and Tunes

SPECIALLY PREPARED FOR THE USE OF

SUNDAY-SCHOOLS

AND FOR

SOCIAL AND FAMILY WORSHIP.

BY
Rev. E. P. PARKER.

THIRD EDITION.

HARTFORD:
HAMERSLEY & CO.
PHILADELPHIA: J. B. LIPPINCOTT & CO.
1871.

Entered according to Act of Congress, in the year 1869, by

E. P. PARKER,

in the Clerk's Office of the District Court of the United States for the District of Connecticut.

ELECTROTYPED BY
MACKELLAR, SMITHS & JORDAN,
PHILADELPHIA.

PREFACE.

The favor with which the "Song-Flower" collection of Sunday School hymns and tunes was received, and also numerous and urgent requests for another similar volume, have induced the preparation of this book. I send it forth, trusting it may find and delight many friends both old and new, and do a good service generally.

That the pages of this volume may not be disfigured and encumbered with personal references, the names of authors are not printed with the tunes and hymns. Besides such information and credit as the index furnishes, special acknowledgments are hereby made, as follows:

From **Songs of Gladness,** by permission.

"Our Song of Triumph," . Page 39, Words and Music by Rev. Alfred Taylor.
"The Other Side," . . . " 52, Music by J. E. Gould, Words by S. L. Cuthbert.
"At the Door," . . . . " 98, " " " " Rev. A. Taylor.

From **Sabbath Songs for Children's Worship,** by permission.

"Pleasant Pastures," Page 43, Music by G. F. Ryder, Words by Rev. E. A. Rand.
"I Need Thee," . . " 93, Music by D. F. Hodges.

From **Songs for the New Life,** by permission of Root & Cady.

"I Love to Hear the Story," Page 65.
"Home Above," . . . . " 67.

From **The Casket,** by permission of Asa D. Hull.

"Altar," . . . . . . Page 82.

PREFACE.

From **Silver Spray,** by permission of W. H. Doane.
"THE JASPER SEA," . . . Page 76.

By permission of Messrs. Bigelow & Main.
"OUR LOVING REDEEMER," Page 30, Music by Wm. B. Bradbury.
"COME SING WITH GLADNESS," " 55.

By permission of the Author.
"LEAD THEM TO THEE," . Page 108, Words and Music by Rev. W. Lowry.
"BEAUTIFUL RIVER," . . " 109, " " " " " "

By permission of Mason Brothers.
"STOCKWELL," . . . . . Page 118, Rev. D. E. Jones.
"FEDERAL ST.," . . . . " 125, H. K. Oliver.

By permission of Wm. Hall & Son.
"INVITATION," . . . . . Page 122, Arranged from Wallace.

By permission of O. Ditson & Co.
"A LAMP UNTO MY FEET," . Page 110, L. O. Emerson.
"STRANGERS AND PILGRIMS," " 111, " "

By the kindness of the author, W. H. Doane.
"WANDERER DO NOT TARRY," Page 89.

By permission of A. S. Barnes & Co.
"DEAR JESUS," . . . . Page 133.

Persons desirous of borrowing from these pages for other collections, or for any public uses, should be careful to obtain permission from the Editor. The authorship of music composed or arranged for this volume, is, in many instances, intentionally withheld.

E. P. PARKER.

HARTFORD, Nov. 1, 1869.

ORDER OF SERVICE FOR CHILDREN ON EACH LORD'S DAY.

1. Singing of Hymn.
2. Responsive Reading of the Psalms, (or Te Deum.)
3. Prayer (closing with the Lord's prayer offered by the whole school.)
4. Singing of Hymn.
5. The Scripture Lesson for the Day.
6. Catechetical Exercises.   (Distribution of Library Books.)
7. Word of Exhortation from Pastor or Superintendent.
8. Singing of Hymn, (or chant.)
9. Benediction.

ORDER OF SERVICE FOR SUNDAY-SCHOOL CONCERT.

1. Sentences from Holy Scriptures, (by the Leader.)
2. Singing of Hymn.
3. Responsive Reading of Te Deum, (or Psalms.)
4. Apostles Creed, (repeated in unison.)
5. Prayer (closing with Lord's prayer in unison.)
6. Singing of Hymn.
7. Children's Scriptural Recitations.
8. Singing of Hymn.
9. Addresses.
10. Hymn or Chant.
11. Benediction.

No. III. JUBILATE DEO.

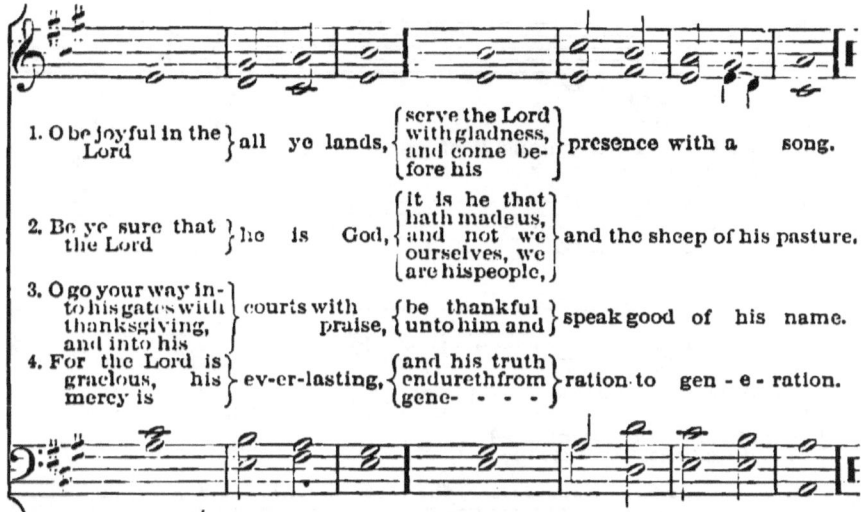

1. O be joyful in the Lord } all ye lands, { serve the Lord with gladness, and come before his } presence with a song.
2. Be ye sure that the Lord } he is God, { it is he that hath made us, and not we ourselves, we are his people, } and the sheep of his pasture.
3. O go your way into his gates with thanksgiving, and into his } courts with praise, { be thankful unto him and } speak good of his name.
4. For the Lord is gracious, his mercy is } ev-er-lasting, { and his truth endureth from gene- - - - } ration to gen-e-ration.

No. IV. BENEDICTUS.

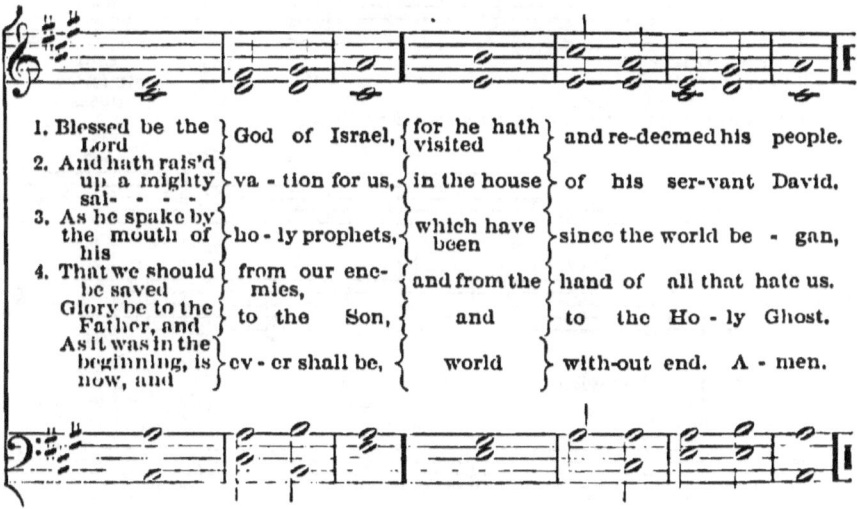

1. Blessed be the Lord } God of Israel, { for he hath visited } and re-deemed his people.
2. And hath rais'd up a mighty sal- - - - } va-tion for us, { in the house } of his ser-vant David.
3. As he spake by the mouth of his } ho-ly prophets, { which have been } since the world be - gan,
4. That we should be saved } from our enemies, { and from the } hand of all that hate us.
    Glory be to the Father, and } to the Son, { and } to the Ho-ly Ghost.
    As it was in the beginning, is now, and } ev-er shall be, { world } with-out end. A - men.

No. VI. BONUM EST. 11

No. VII. DEUS MISEREATUR.

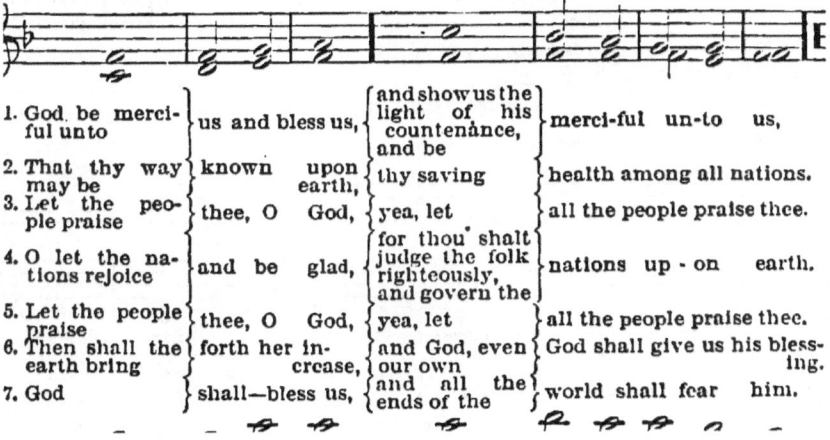

No. IX. LAUDATE DOMINUM.

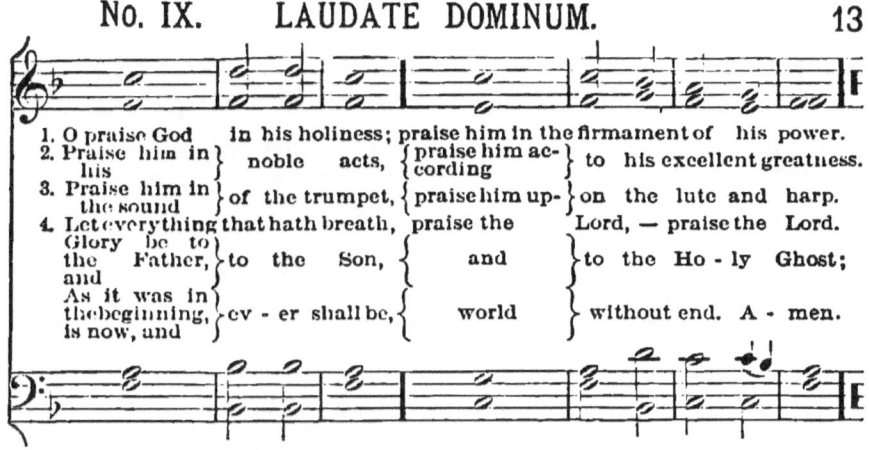

No. X. O SAVIOUR OF THE WORLD.

No. XI. GLORIA IN EXCELSIS.

No. XII.   TE DEUM LAUDAMUS.

We praise thee, O God; we acknowledge thee to be the Lord;
All the earth doth worship thee, the Father everlasting.
To thee all angels cry aloud; the heavens and all the powers therein;
To thee cherubim and seraphim continually do cry,—
Holy, holy, holy Lord God of Sabaoth!
Heaven and earth are full of the majesty of thy glory.
The glorious company of the apostles praise thee!
The goodly fellowship of the prophets praise thee!
The noble army of martyrs praise thee!
The holy church throughout all the world doth acknowledge thee,—
The Father, of an infinite majesty;
Thine adorable, true, and only Son; also the Holy Ghost, the Comforter.
Thou art the King of glory, O Christ;
Thou art the everlasting Son of the Father.
When thou tookest upon thee to deliver man,
Thou didst humble thyself to be born of a virgin.
When thou hadst overcome the sharpness of death,
Thou didst open the kingdom of heaven to all believers.
Thou sittest at the right hand of God, in the glory of the Father.
We believe that thou shalt come to be our Judge.
We therefore pray thee, help thy servants whom thou hast redeemed with thy precious blood;
Make them to be numbered with thy saints in glory everlasting.
O Lord, save thy people, and bless thine heritage;
Govern them and lift them up forever.
Day by day we magnify thee,
And we worship thy name ever, world without end.
Vouchsafe, O Lord, to keep us this day without sin.
O Lord, have mercy upon us; have mercy upon us.
O Lord let thy mercy be upon us, as our trust is in thee.
O Lord, in thee have I trusted; let me never be confounded.

No. XIII. THE APOSTLES' CREED.

I BELIEVE in God, the Father Almighty, Maker of heaven and earth; and in Jesus Christ, his only Son, our Lord, who was conceived by the Holy Ghost, born of the Virgin Mary, suffered under Pontius Pilate, was crucified, dead, and buried. He descended into hell [Hades]; the third day he arose again from the dead; he ascended into heaven, and sitteth on the right hand of God, the Father Almighty: from thence he shall come to judge the quick and the dead.

I believe in the Holy Ghost; the holy catholic church; the communion of saints; the forgiveness of sins; the resurrection of the body, and the life everlasting. Amen.

THE LORD'S PRAYER.

Our Father which art in heaven, hallowed be thy name; thy kingdom come; thy will be done in earth as it is in heaven. Give us this day our daily bread. And forgive our debts as we forgive our debtors. And lead us not into temptation, but deliver us from evil. For thine is the kingdom, and the power, and the glory forever. Amen.

CHRISTMAS CAROL. 17

1. God rest ye, all good people, let nothing you dismay; For Jesus Christ, your Saviour was born on Christmas day; The dawn rose red o'er Bethlehem, and stars shone through the gray, When Jesus Christ, our Saviour, was born on Christmas day.

2. God rest ye, little children, let nothing you affright,
For Jesus Christ, your Saviour, was born this happy night;
Along the hills of Galilee the white flocks sleeping lay,
When Christ, the child of Nazareth, was born on Christmas day.

3. God rest ye, all good Christians, upon this blessed morn,
The Lord of all good Christians was of a woman born;
Now all your sorrows he doth heal, your sins he takes away,
For Jesus Christ, our Saviour, was born on Christmas day.

CHRISTMAS SONG.

1. Calm, on the list'ning ear of night, Come heaven's melodious strains, Where wild Ju-de-a stretches far Her sil-ver-mantled plains. And angels, with their sparkling lyres, Make mus-ic on the air. Ce-lestial choirs, from courts above, 'Mid sa-cred glo-ries there;

2. The answering hills of Palestine
    Send back the glad reply;
   And greet, from all their holy
      heights,
    The dayspring from on high.
   O'er the blue depths of Galilee
    There comes a holier calm;
   And Sharon waves, in solemn
      praise,
    Her silent groves of palm.

3. "Glory to God!" the sounding skies
    Loud with their anthems ring;
   "Peace to the earth—good will to
      men,
    From heaven's eternal King."
   Light on thy hills, Jerusalem!
    The Saviour now is born!
   And bright on Bethlehem's joyous
      plains
    Breaks the first Christmas morn.

BRIGHEST AND BEST.

2. Cold on his cradle the dew-drops are shining;
 Low lies his head, with the beasts of the stall;
 Angels adore him in slumber reclining—
 Maker, and Monarch, and Saviour of all.

3. Say, shall we yield him, in costly devotion,
 Odors of Edom, and offerings divine?
 Gems of the mountain, and pearls of the ocean,
 Myrrh from the forest, or gold from the mine?

4. Vainly we offer each ample oblation,
 Vainly with gold would his favor secure:
 Richer, by far, is the heart's adoration,—
 Dearer to God are the prayers of the poor.

3. Chant him, ye laughing flowers,
    Fresh from the sod;
  Chant him, wild leaping streams,
    Praising your God.
  Break from *thy* winter,
    Sad heart, and sing!
  Bud with thy blossoms fair;
    Christ is thy spring.

4. Come where the Lord hath lain,
    Past is the gloom;
  See the full eye of day
    Smile through the tomb!
  Hark! angel voices
    Fall from the skies!
  Christ hath arisen!
    Glad hearts, arise!

RESURRECTION HYMN. 21

1. Al - le - lu - ia! Al - le - lu - ia! Hearts to heav'n and voi-ces raise;
Sing to God a hymn of gladness, Sing to God a hymn of praise;
He, who on the cross a vic-tim, For the world's sal-va-tion bled,
Je - sus Christ, the King of glo - ry, Now is ris - en from the dead.

2. Christ is risen, Christ the first-fruits
Of the holy harvest-field,
Which will all its full abundance
At his second coming yield;
Then the golden ears of harvest
Will their heads before him wave,
Ripened by his glorious sunshine
From the furrows of the grave.

3. Christ is risen; we are risen;
Shed upon us heavenly grace,
Rain, and dew, and gleams of glory
From the brightness of thy face,
That we, with our hearts in heaven,
Here on earth may fruitful be,
And by angel-hands be gathered,
And be ever, Lord, with thee.

22. HOLY SAVIOUR, PRAY FOR ME.

1. O holy Saviour, pray for me, While far from heaven and thee, I wander in a fragile bark, O'er life's tempestuous sea.

Chorus.—O Saviour dear, remember me, And never cease thy care, Till, in the realms above the sky, Thy love and bliss I share.

Then blessed Jesus, from thy throne, So bright in bliss above; Protect thy child in virtue's path, With thy bright smile of love.

2. Where rude temptations try my heart,
And pleasure spreads her snare,
Thy loving aid shall heal the smart,
And show a Saviour's care;
Then blessed Jesus, be thou kind,
And listen to my prayer;
In all my troubles may I find
And feel thy tender care.

GOOD TIDINGS.

23

1. All my heart this night re-joi-ces, As I hear, far and near,
Sweet-est an-gel voi-ces, "Christ is born!" their choirs are singing,
Till the air, ev'-rywhere Now with joy is ring-ing.

2. Hark! a voice from yond-er manger, Soft and sweet, doth entreat,
"Flee from woe and dan-ger; Brethren, come, from all that grieves you,
You are freed; all you need I will sure-ly give you."

3. Blessed Saviour, let me find thee!
Keep thou me close to thee,
Cast me not behind thee:
Life of life, my heart thou stillest,
Calm I rest on thy breast,
All this void thou fillest.

4. Come, then, let us hasten yonder;
Here let all, great and small,
Kneel in awe and wonder;
Love him who with love is yearning,
Hail the star, that from far,
Bright with hope is burning.

CHILD'S DESIRE.

1. I think, when I read that sweet sto-ry of old, When Je-sus was here among men, How he called little children as lambs to his fold, I should like to have been with him then.

2. I wish that his hands had been placed on my head,
That his arm had been thrown around me,
And that I might have seen his kind look when he said,
"Let the little ones come unto me."

3. Yet still to his footstool in prayer I may go,
And ask for a share in his love;
And if I thus earnestly seek him below,
I shall see him and hear him above;

4. In that beautiful place he has gone to prepare
For all who are washed and forgiven,
And many dear children are gathering there,
"For of such is the kingdom of heaven."

BRIGHTLY GLEAMS OUR BANNER.—Concluded.

Brightly gleams our banner, Pointing to the sky, Waving wand'rers onward, To their home on high.

WATCH AND PRAY.

1. "Christian, seek not yet re-pose!" Hear thy guardian an-gel say;
2. Hear the vic-tors who o'ercame; Still they mark each warrior's way;

Thou art in the midst of foes,—"Watch and pray!"
All with one sweet voice ex-claim, "Watch and pray!"

3. Hear the warning of thy Lord,
   Him thou lovest to obey;
   Hide within thy heart his word,—
   "Watch and pray!"

4. Watch, as if on that alone
   Hung the issue of the day;
   Pray, that help may be sent down;
   "Watch and pray!"

28. O'ER THE SILENT RIVER.

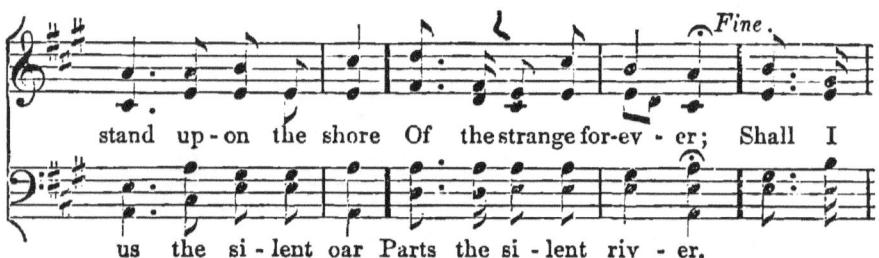
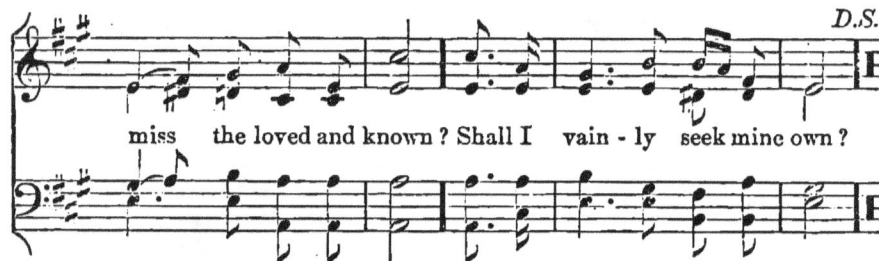

1. When for me the silent oar Parts the silent river; And I stand upon the shore Of the strange forever; Shall I miss the loved and known? Shall I vainly seek mine own?

   Chorus.—When for us the silent oar Parts the silent river.

2. Can the bonds that make us here
   Know ourselves immortal,
   Drop away, like foliage sere,
   At life's inner portal?
   What is holiest here below,
   Must forever live and grow.—Cho.

3. He who on our earthly path
   Bids us help each other,
   Who his well-beloved hath
   Made our elder brother,
   Will but clasp the chain of love
   Closer when we meet above.—Cho.

4. Therefore do not dread to go
   O'er the silent river;
   Death, thy hastening oar I know;
   Bear me, thou life-giver,
   Through the waters, to the shore,
   Where mine own have gone before.
   Chorus.

HARK! THE SONGS OF ZION. 29

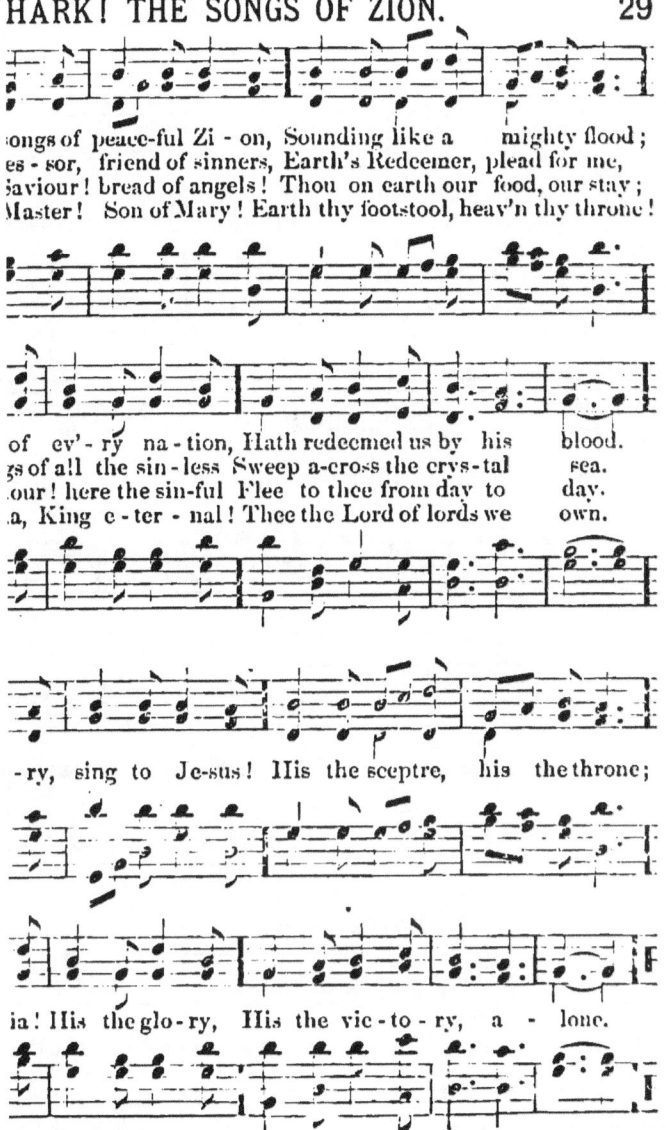

2. Our sins, though as scarlet, they all shall be clean,
Washed white in thy blood, as the beautiful snow;
The robe of thy righteousness on us be seen,
The joy of forgiveness our young hearts shall know.
  We come, oh, &c.
Our peace, like a river, unbroken shall flow.

3. When life is all over, we hope then above,—
Where cometh no terror, where falleth no tear,
To sing in sweet numbers thy wonderful love,
With all who in childhood have followed thee here.
  We come, oh, &c.
In the glory of heaven at last to appear.

THY WILL BE DONE.

1. My God, my Father, while I stray Far from my home on life's rough way;
2. Though dark my path and sad my lot, Let me be still and mur-mur not,
3. If thou should'st call me to re - sign What most I prize, it ne'er was mine;
4. Let but my fainting heart be blest With thy sweet Spirit for its guest,
5. Renew my will from day to - day, Blend it with thine, and take a - way

A - men.

1. O teach me from my heart to say, Thy will be done.
2. Or breathe the prayer di- vine - ly taught,
3. I only yield thee what is thine,
4. My God to thee I leave the rest;
5. All that now makes it hard to say, Thy will be done.

A - men.

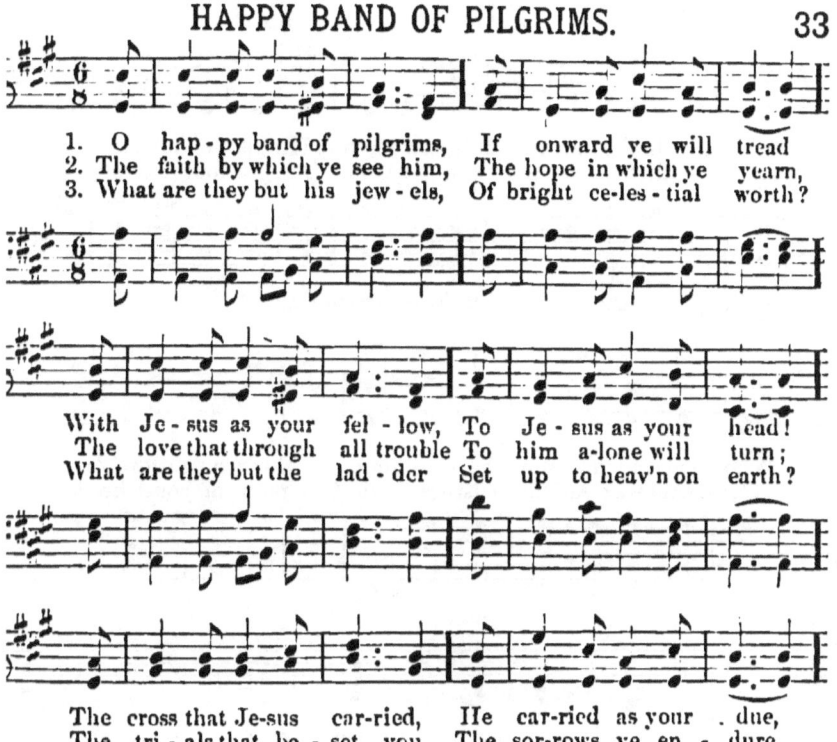

VIENNA.

1. Heavenly Father, send thy blessing On thy children gathered here; May they all, thy name confessing, Be to thee forever dear; May they be like Joseph, loving, Dutiful and chaste and pure; And their faith like David proving, Steadfast unto death endure.

2. Holy Saviour, who in meekness
   Didst vouchsafe a child to be,
   Guide their steps and help their
     weakness,
   Bless and make them like to thee;
   Bear thy lambs when they are weary
     In thine arms, and at thy breast;
   Through life's desert, dry and dreary,
     Bring them to thy heavenly rest.

3. Spread thy golden pinions o'er them,
     Holy Spirit, Heavenly Dove,
   Guide them, lead them, go before
     them,
   Give them peace, and joy, and love.
   Temples of the Holy Spirit,
     May they with thy glory shine,
   And immortal bliss inherit,
     And for evermore be thine!

INTERCESSION.—Concluded.

Hear then, in love, O Lord, the cry, In heav'n thy dwell-ing-place on high.

JESUS, TENDER SAVIOUR.

1. Je-sus, ten-der Sa-viour! Hast thou died for me?
Make me ve-ry thank-ful, In my heart to thee.

2. When the sad, sad story
Of thy grief I read,
For my sins, oh, make me
Penitent indeed.

3. Soon I hope, in glory,
At thy side to stand;
Make me fit to meet thee,
In that happy land.

COME, LITTLE CHILDREN, COME.

1. Come, little children, come, The Saviour calls you near; He'll tell you of his heav'nly home, And gently lead you there.

2. Haste, little children, haste,
   To be the Saviour's lambs;
   Come, of his loving-kindness taste,
   And nestle in his arms.

3. Try, little children, try,
   To love the Saviour well,

Who left his home above the sky,
To save your souls from hell.

4. Pray, little children, pray,
   That you may be forgiven;
   And ask that God will lead the way
   To Jesus Christ and heaven.

SHEPHERD-CALL.

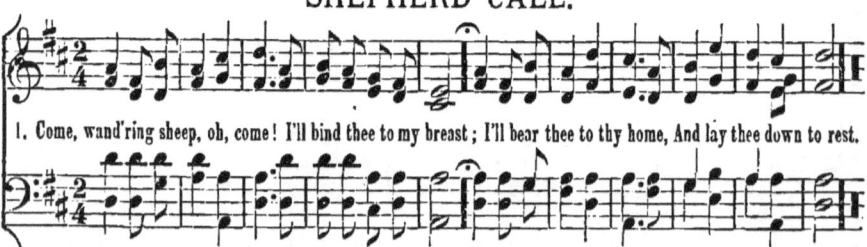

1. Come, wand'ring sheep, oh, come! I'll bind thee to my breast; I'll bear thee to thy home, And lay thee down to rest.

2. I saw thee stray forlorn;
   I heard thee faintly cry;
   And on the tree of scorn
   For thee I deigned to die.

3. I shield thee from alarms,
   And wilt thou not be blest?
   I bear thee in my arms,
   Thou, bear me in thy breast.

HOW LOVING IS JESUS.

1. How loving is Jesus, who came from the sky, In tenderest pity for sinners to die; His hands and his feet they were nail'd to the tree, And all this he suffered for sinners like me, And all this he suffered for sinners like me.

2. How gladly does Jesus free pardon impart To all who receive him by faith in the heart! No evil befals them, their home is above, And Jesus throws round them the arms of his love, And Jesus throws round them the arms of his love.

3. Oh, give then to Jesus your earliest days; They only are blessed who walk in his ways; In life and in death he will still be their friend; For those whom he loves he will love to the end, For those whom he loves he will love to the end.

ONE BY ONE.

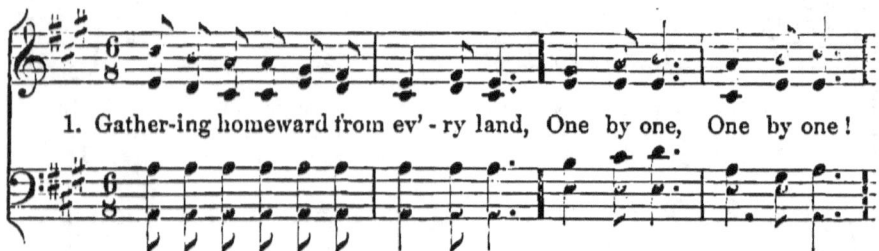

1. Gathering homeward from ev'-ry land, One by one, One by one!

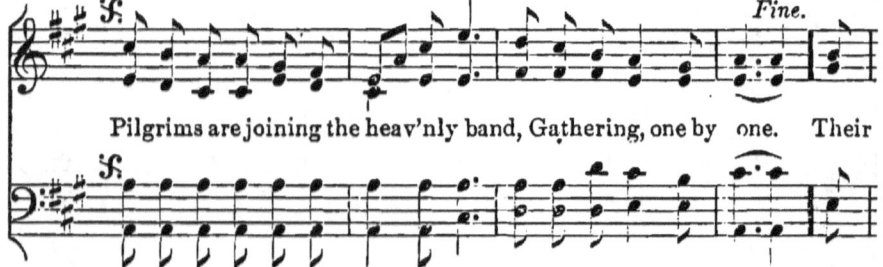

Pilgrims are joining the heav'nly band, Gathering, one by one. Their

Cho.—Gathering homeward from ev'ry land, Gathering, one by one.

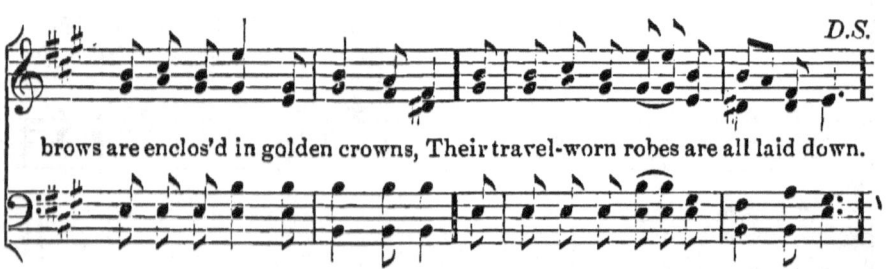

brows are enclos'd in golden crowns, Their travel-worn robes are all laid down.

2. We, too, shall come to the river-side,
   One by one, one by one!
  Nearer its waters each even-tide,
   Gathering, one by one!
  O Jesus, our fainting strength uphold,
  The waves of that river are dark and cold.—Cho.

3. Jesus, Redeemer, be thou our stay—
   One by one, one by one!
  Cross the dark river with us, we pray,
   Gathering, one by one!
  Then boldly we'll come to Jordan's side,
  And fearlessly enter its swelling tide.—Cho.

PLEASANT PASTURES.

1. Pleasant are the pastures where Jesus feeds his flock, Underneath the shadow of the rock; See the Shepherd standing—how gracious is his mien! Standing, waiting, to admit us in.
2. Pleasant are the pastures, all echo-ing with song, Where the living waters glide along; There in peace reposing upon the flow'ry banks, Staying with the Shepherd, we'll sing thanks.

CHORUS.

Sheep of his pasture, there at his side, 'Neath his protection, safe abide; Lost sheep now wand'ring, thither repair; Evil cannot harm you, cannot harm you there.

3. Faithful is the Shepherd, who careth for the sheep;
Never do his eyelids close to sleep;
All his flock he knoweth, and calleth them by name;
And his love is constantly the same.

4. Blessed are the weak ones, who on his arms repose,
Fearing not the fierceness of their foes;
They shall grow and flourish, who in their Lord abide,
Like the trees that grow by rivers' side.

HOME-RETURNING.

1. Yes, kind Saviour, grieving O'er the sad past; All my vain hopes leaving, Come I at last. Thine, thine I am, O bleeding Lamb; To thy heart receiving, Hold thou me fast.

2. On thy word re-ly-ing, Safe let me rest; All my tears now drying On thy dear breast. Dawns the sweet day, Bright o'er my way, Foes and fears all flying, Here am I blest.

3. All my footsteps heeding,
Shield me from ill;
In green pastures feeding,
By waters still;
Always with thee,
Lord, let me be;
Thou all kindly leading,
Thine be my will.

4. When—life's last day ending—
Dark death is nigh,
Jesus, o'er me bending,
Note my last sigh.
In that dread hour,
Strong in thy power,
On swift wing ascending,
Home let me fly!

THE VOICE OF THE SAVIOUR.

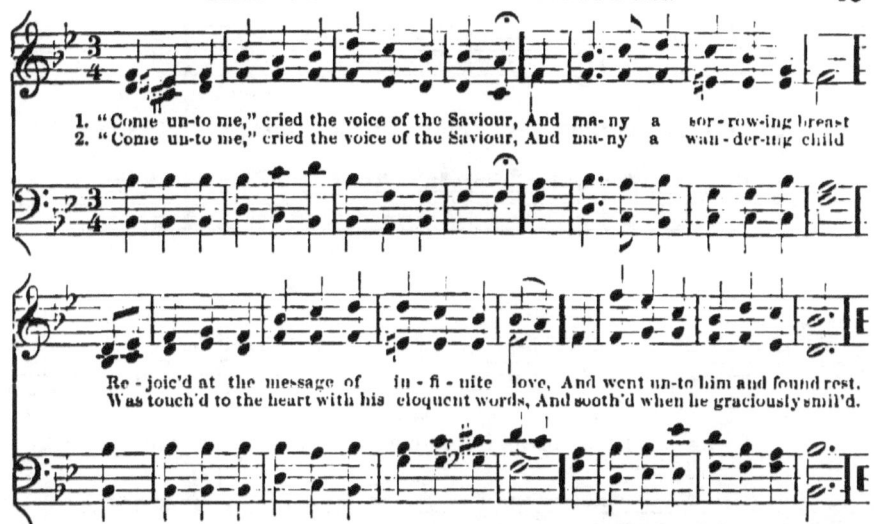

3. "Come unto me," cries the voice of the Saviour,
The Bible re-echoes the cry;
And all through the world the kind message is sent,
"Come, children, for why will ye die?"

4. "Come," cries the voice of the Bride and the Spirit:
Then why should we longer delay?
O now let us hear thy voice speaking to us,
And come to thee, Jesus, to-day.

THE PRAYER.

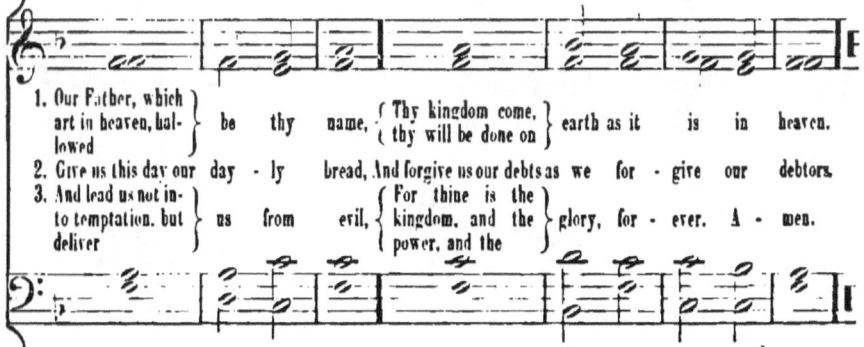

JESUS, MOST HOLY.

1. Jesus, most holy, Pray I to thee; My sinful fetters, Lord, break from me; Take this sad spirit, Mourning for sin, Back to thy bosom,—Lord, take me in!

2. Over the mountains,
    Long have I strayed;
Cold winds of sorrow
    Round me have played;
None to bring comfort,
    None have I found;
While tears of anguish
    Watered the ground.

3. To this dear refuge
    Now have I fled;
Jesus, thy kind heart
    For me hath bled;
Take now the wanderer
    Home to thy rest,
Under thy kind wings,
    Sheltered and blest.

FAST FADES THE DAY.

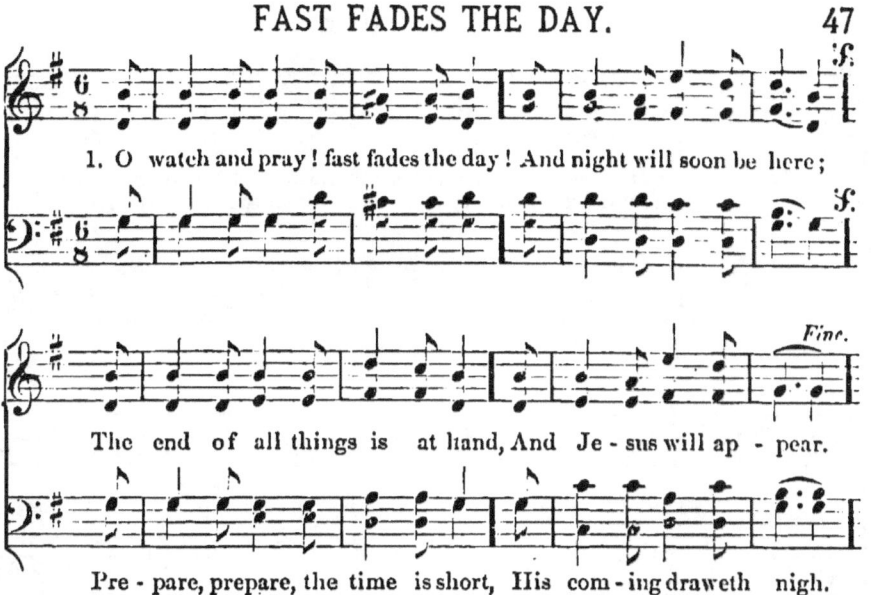

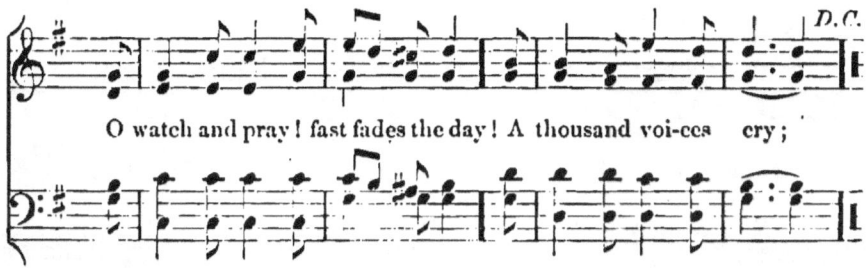

2. O watch and pray! fast fades the day,
   And work is to be done;
   The harvest must be gathered in
   While lasts the summer sun.
   O watch and pray! fast fades the day,
   And what a long, dark night,
   For those who cannot meet the Lord
   And hail him with delight.

3. O watch and pray! say, children, say,
   Are you prepared for home?
   And can you cry with voice of joy,
   "O come, dear Jesus, come?"
   Then watch and pray! fast fades the day!
   O cry, while yet there's time,
   "Lord Jesus, take my sins away,
   And make me wholly thine!"

GERMAN TUNE.

1. Bless-ed Je-sus, gra-cious Saviour, List-en while we sing:
Hearts and voi-ces glad-ly rais-ing Prai-ses to our King.
All we have to thee we of-fer, All we are and hope to be;
Thine are bo-dy, soul, and spi-rit, All we yield to thee.

2. Clearer still, and ever clearer,
Dawns a light from heaven,
Bringing to us in our sadness
News of sin forgiven.
Time for us will soon be over,
Toil and sorrow soon be past;
May we, with thee, blessed Saviour,
Find a rest at last.

3. Onward then, and ever onward
In the upward road,
Trod by holy men before us,
Journeying home to God.
Leaving all the world behind us,
Let us eagerly press on,
Halting not, not looking backward
Till the prize is won.

THE BETTER WORLD.

49

SONG TO THE SAVIOUR.

1. Cre - a - tor, Pre-ser-ver, Re-deem-er of men, Di-vine In-ter-ces-sor a-bove, Oh, where shall the song of thy prai-ses be-gin, Or how shall I speak of thy love? Hea-ven is tell-ing, And earth is re-veal-ing, What won-ders thy mer-cy can prove.

2. And do I not love thee, O Saviour di-vine, The chief of ten thousands to me? Yes, in-fi-nite beau-ty and glo-ry are thine, Whose brightness no mor-tal can see. An-gels shall bless thee, And men shall con-fess thee; All worlds shall ac-know-ledge thy sway.

3. Thine, thine is the kingdom, the wisdom and pow'r, The glo-ry and hon-or supreme; For ev-er and ev-er my soul would a-dore The un-speak-a-ble worth of thy name! For ev-er and ever, O glo-ri-ous Sa-viour, I'll dwell on the rap-tu-rous theme.

MY HEART IS RESTING.

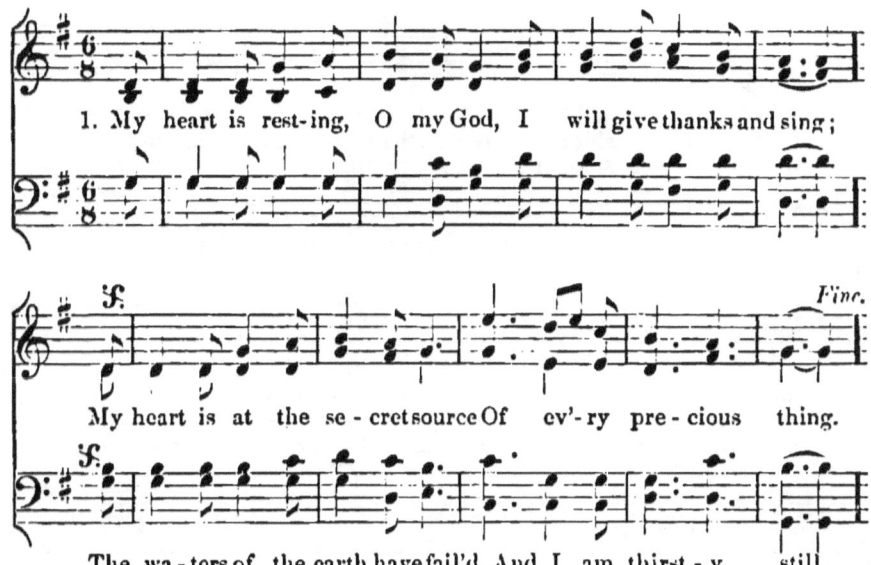

1. My heart is rest-ing, O my God, I will give thanks and sing;
My heart is at the se-cret source Of ev'-ry pre-cious thing.
The wa-ters of the earth have fail'd, And I am thirst-y still.
Now the frail ves-sel thou hast made, No hand but thine shall fill;

2. I thirst for springs of heav'nly life,
And here all day they rise;
I seek the treasure of thy love,
And close at hand it lies.
I have a heritage of joy
That yet I cannot see;
The hand that bled to make it mine,
Is keeping it for me.

3. My heart is resting, O my God,
My heart is in thy care;
I hear the voice of joy and health
Resounding everywhere.
"Thou art my portion," saith my soul,
Ten thousand voices say!
And the music of their glad Amen
Shall never die away.

HE LEADETH ME.

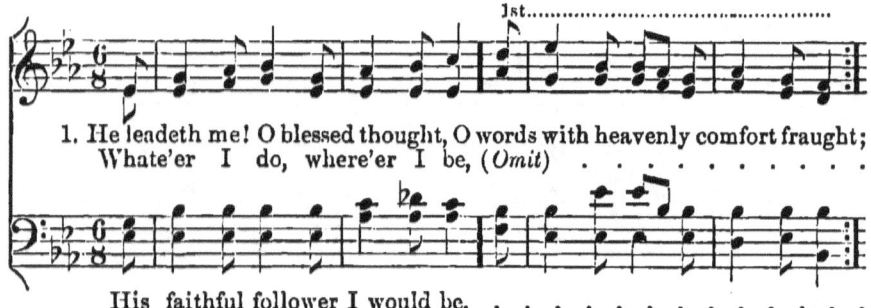

1. He leadeth me! O blessed thought, O words with heavenly comfort fraught;
Whate'er I do, where'er I be, (*Omit*) . . . .
His faithful follower I would be, ...

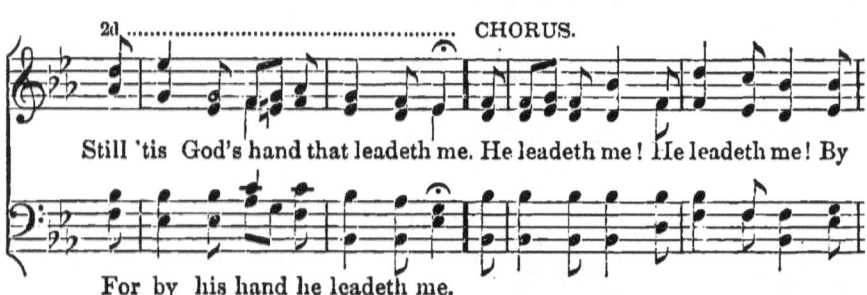

Still 'tis God's hand that leadeth me. He leadeth me! He leadeth me! By
For by his hand he leadeth me.

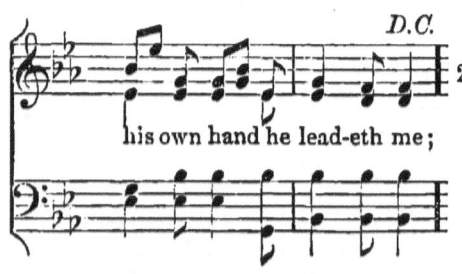

his own hand he lead-eth me;

2. Sometimes 'mid scenes of deepest gloom,
Sometimes where Eden's bowers bloom,
By waters still, o'er troubled sea—
Still 'tis his hand that leadeth me!—
Cho.

3. Lord, I would clasp thy hand in mine,
Nor ever murmur nor repine—
Content, whatever lot I see,
Since 'tis my God that leadeth me.—Cho.

4. And when my task on earth is done,
When, by thy grace, the victory's won,
E'en death's cold wave I will not flee,
Since God through Jordan leadeth me.—Cho.

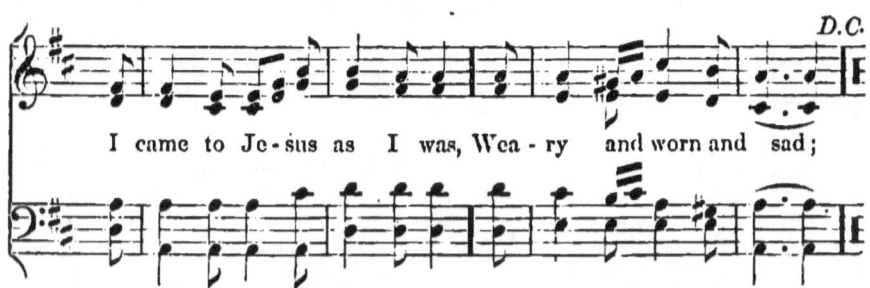

2. I heard the voice of Jesus say,
   "Behold, I freely give
   The living water! thirsty one,
   Stoop down, and drink, and live."
   I came to Jesus, and I drank
   Of that life-giving stream;
   My thirst was quenched, my soul re-
   And now I live in him. [vived,

3. I heard the voice of Jesus say,
   "I am this dark world's light:
   Look unto me; thy morn shall rise,
   And all thy day be bright."
   I looked to Jesus and I found,
   In him my Star, my Sun;
   And in that light of life I'll walk
   Till all my journey's done.

COME, JESUS, REDEEMER. 59

1. Come, Jesus, Redeemer, abide thou with me; Come, gladden my spirit that waiteth for thee; Thy smile ev'ry shadow shall chase from my heart, And soothe every sorrow, tho' keen be the smart.

2. Thy love, oh, how faithful, so tender, so pure,
Thy promise, faith's anchor, how steadfast and sure!
That love, like sweet sunshine, my cold heart can warm,
That promise make steady my soul in the storm.

3. Breathe, breathe on my spirit, oft ruffled, thy peace;
From restless, vain wishes, bid thou my heart cease;
In thee all its longings henceforward shall end,
Till, glad, to thy presence my soul shall ascend.

ART THOU WEARY?

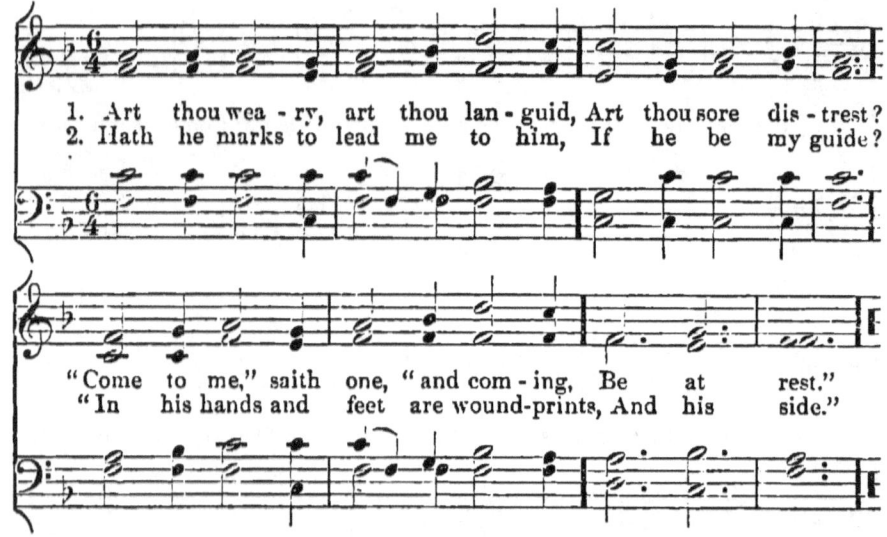

1. Art thou wea-ry, art thou lan-guid, Art thou sore dis-trest?
2. Hath he marks to lead me to him, If he be my guide?

"Come to me," saith one, "and com-ing, Be at rest."
"In his hands and feet are wound-prints, And his side."

3. If I find him, if I follow,
   What his guerdon here?
   "Many a sorrow, many a labor,
   Many a tear."

4. If I ask him to receive me,
   Will he say me nay?
   "Not till earth, and not till heaven,
   Pass away."

THE SAVIOUR'S CALL. 6s & 4s.

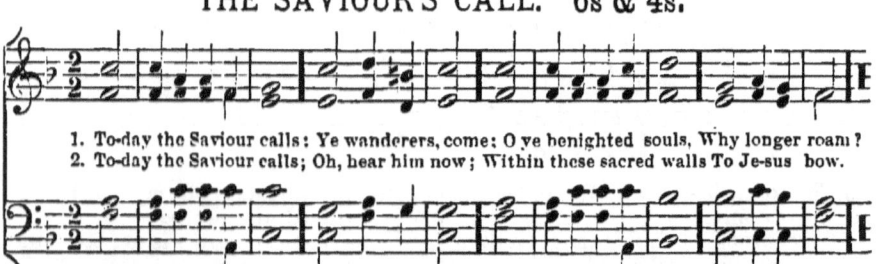

1. To-day the Saviour calls: Ye wanderers, come: O ye benighted souls, Why longer roam?
2. To-day the Saviour calls; Oh, hear him now; Within these sacred walls To Je-sus bow.

3. To-day the Saviour calls;
   For refuge fly;
   The storm of justice falls,
   And death is nigh.

4. The Spirit calls to-day;
   Yield to his power;
   Oh, grieve him not away:
   'Tis mercy's hour.

BEAUTIFUL LAND OF REST.

1. Je - ru - sa-lem, so bright and fair, Beau-ti-ful land of rest!
No gloomy night, nor sor - row there, Beau-ti-ful land of rest!
Je - sus, the Sun, for - ev - er reigns O'er all those bright celestial plains,
And an - gels sing in joy - ful strains, In the land of rest.

2. We long to see thy pearly gates,
 Beautiful land of rest!
And for their opening still we wait,
 Beautiful land of rest!
And when our toils and cares are o'er,
 Then those who've crossed the stream before
Will welcome us to Canaan's shore,
 To the land of rest!

3. Unto the river's banks we come,
 Beautiful land of rest!
Each moment brings us nearer home,
 Beautiful land of rest!
There millions who've the victory found,
 Have laid the cross and armor down,
But we are striving for the crown,
 In the land of rest!

COME, YE FAITHFUL. 63

1. Come, ye faith-ful, raise the strain Of tri-umph-ant glad-ness;
2. 'Tis the spring of souls to-day, Christ hath burst his pri-son;

Cho.—Al-le-lu-ia, with the Son, God the Fa-ther praising;

God had brought his Is-ra-el In-to joy from sad-ness.
And from three days' sleep in death As a sun hath ri-sen.

Al-le-lu-ia yet a-gain To the Spi-rit rais-ing.

Al-le-lu-ia now we cry To our King im-mor-tal,
All the win-ter of our sins, Long and dark, is fly-ing

Who tri-umph-ant burst the bars Of the tomb's dark por-tal.
From his light, to whom we give Laud and praise un-dy-ing.

FLEE AS A BIRD.

1. Flee as a bird to your mountain, Thou who art weary of sin;
Go to the clear flowing fountain, (*Omit*) . . . .
Where you may wash and be clean. Fly, for th' aven-ger is near thee;
Call, and the Sa-viour will hear thee; He on his bo-som will bear thee,— O thou who art wea-ry of sin.

2. He will pro-tect thee for-ev-er, Wipe every sad falling tear,
He will for-sake thee, oh, never, (*Omit*) . . . .
Cherished so ten-der-ly there; Haste, then, the hours now are flying;
Spend not the mo-ments in sigh-ing; Cease from your sorrow and cry-ing, The Sa-viour will wipe ev'-ry tear.

JESUS, STILL LEAD ON.

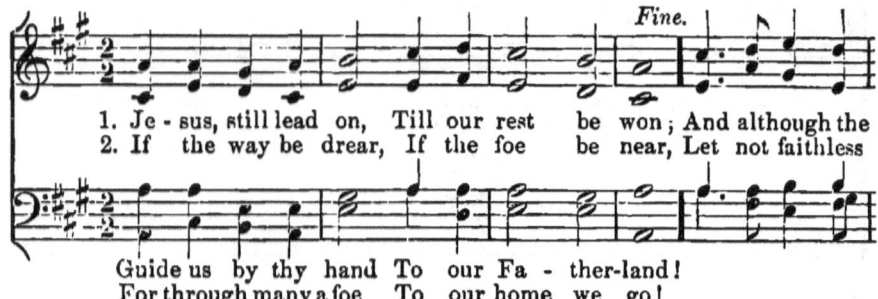

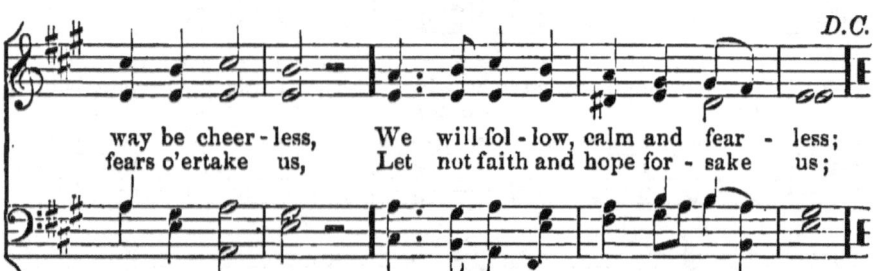

3. When we seek relief
   From a long-felt grief;
   When temptations come alluring,
   Make us patient and enduring:
   Show us that bright shore
   Where we weep no more!

4. Jesus, still lead on,
   Till our rest be won;
   Heavenly Leader, still direct us,
   Still support, console, protect us,
   Till we safely stand
   In our Fatherland!

GENTLE SHEPHERD.

HOME ABOVE.

1. Oh, how my spi-rit longs for thee, Beau-ti-ful home a-bove.
Where I may rest from sor-row free, Beau-ti-ful home a-bove.
With-in the gold-en gates of light, Arrayed in garments pure and white,
I'll walk with an-gels fair and bright, (*Omit*) . . . .
In my home a-bove. :||: Beau-ti-ful home a-bove, :||: Oh,
come and take me, Saviour, come, To my beau-ti-ful home a-bove.

2. To reach thee safe I daily pray,
  Beautiful home above.
And travel in the toilsome way,
  Beautiful home above.
My weary feet are bruised and sore;
But Jesus' feet were bruised before,
To bring me to the open door
  Of my beautiful home.—Cho.

THE LOVE OF JESUS.

1. There is no love like the love of Je-sus, Nev-er to fade or fall,
2. There is no heart like the heart of Je-sus, Fill'd with a tender lore,
3. There is no voice like the voice of Je-sus; Ah, how sweet its chime!
4. O might we list-en that voice of Je-sus, O might we nev-er roam,

Till in-to the fold of the peace of God, He has gathered us all.
Not a throb or a throe our hearts can know, But he suffered before.
Like the musical ring of some rushing spring In the sum-mer time.
Till our souls should rest in peace on his breast In the hea-ven-ly home.

Chorus.—No love like the love of Je - sus, Nev-er to fade or fall,
Till in - to the fold of the peace of God, He has gathered us all.

LIGHT FROM HEAVEN.

1. While on life's stormy sea My bark is driven; From a far coast to me Sweet light is giv'n: Gleaming a-round my way, Chang-ing dark night to day; Blend-ing its gold-en ray With hues of heav'n.

2. That beacon light I have,
  And lose all fear;
The Saviour walks the wave,
  His voice I hear:
My perfect, precious guide,
Bidding the storm subside,
Showing beyond the tide,
  Skies heavenly clear.

3. I feel thy magnet powers,
  Bright world to come!
Faith sees thy glorious bowers
  Where angels roam:
Where loved ones, gone before,
Now beckon from the shore,
And make me long the more
  For them and home.

SAVIOUR, LEAD US.

1. Saviour, like a Shepherd lead us, Much we need thy tender care:
In thy pleasant pastures feed us, For our use thy folds prepare;
Blessed Jesus! Blessed Jesus! Thou hast bought us, thine we are.

2. Thou hast promised to receive us,
  Poor and sinful though we be;
 Thou hast mercy to relieve us,
  Grace to cleanse and power to free:
   :||: Blessed Jesus! :||:
 Let us early turn to thee.

3. Early let us seek thy favor;
  Early let us learn thy will;
 Do thou, Lord, our only Saviour,
  With thy love our bosoms fill:
   :||: Blessed Jesus! :||:
 Thou hast loved us,—love us still!

CRUSADER'S HYMN.

1. Fair-est Lord Je-sus! Ru-ler of all na-ture! O thou of God and man the Son! Thee will I cher-ish; Thee will I hon-or; Thou, my soul's glo-ry, joy, and crown.

2. Fair are the meadows, fairer still the woodlands,
   Robed in the blooming garb of spring:
   Jesus is fairer, Jesus is purer,
     Who makes the woeful heart to sing.

3. Fair is the sunshine, fairer still the moonshine,
   And the twinkling starry host:
   Jesus shines fairer, Jesus shines purer,
     Than all the angels heaven can boast.

₊ *The hymn and music said to be found in the helmet of a Crusader.*

3. In the weary hours of sickness,
   In the days of grief and pain,
   When we feel our mortal weakness,
   When the creature's help is vain,
       By thy mercy, &c.

4. In the solemn hour of dying,
   In the awful judgment-day,
   May our souls, on thee relying,
   Find thee still our hope and stay.
       By thy mercy, &c.

76. THE JASPER SEA.

1. When we've cross'd the Jasper sea To the oth-er shore;
Full of bliss our songs shall be, Prais-ing ev-er-more.

2. With the an-gels round the throne, Rob'd in white we'll stand;
Death and tears are nev-er known In that hap-py land.

3. Part-ing days will nev-er come; Bright our lot will be,
When we reach our heav'n-ly home O'er the Jas-per sea.

CHORUS.

When we cross the shore Of the Jas-per sea, Joy shall reign for-ev-ermore, And heav'n our home shall be, And heav'n our home shall be.

JESUS WAITING TO ENTER. 77

1. O Je-sus, thou art stand-ing Out-side the fast-clos'd door;
In low-ly patience wait-ing To pass the threshold o'er:

Shame on us, Chris-tian breth-ren, His name and sign who

bear, Oh, shame, thrice shame upon us To keep him stand-ing there.

2. O Jesus, thou art knocking;
    And lo! that hand is scarred,
And thorns thy brow encircle,
    And tears thy face have marred;
Oh, love that passeth knowledge,
    So patiently to wait;
Oh, sin that hath no equal,
    So fast to bar the gate!

3. O Jesus, thou art pleading
    In accents meek and low,
"I died for you, my children,
    And will ye treat me so?"
O Lord, with shame and sorrow
    We open now the door;
Dear Saviour, enter, enter,
    And leave us nevermore.

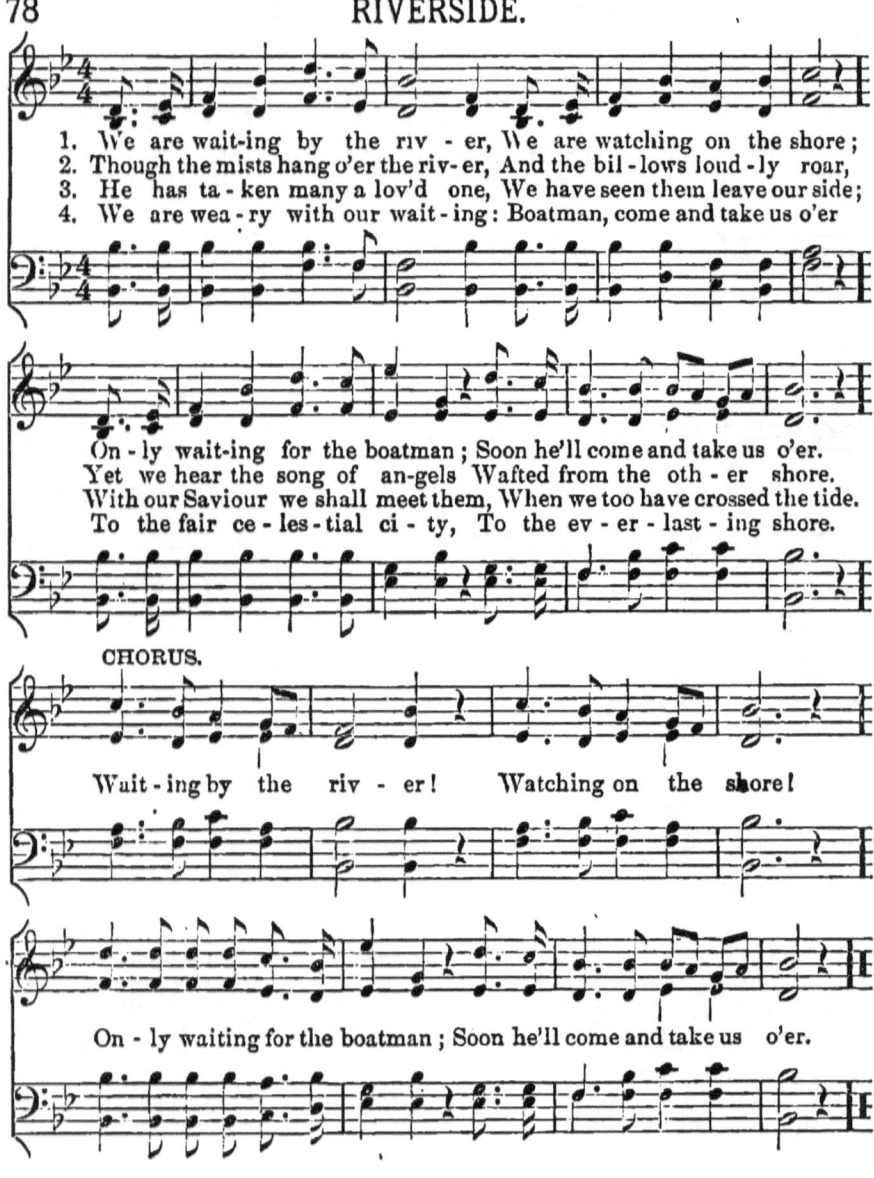

HOME OF THE SOUL.

1. Beau-ti-ful Si-on, the home of the soul! Ev-ermore longing for thee;
2. Fond-ly we cherish our hope of thy rest; Bravely toil on to the goal;
3. Dear na-tive country, oh blessed will be Rest on thy sweet-sounding shore;

Wayworn and weary, still onward we press Thy joy and thy glo-ry to see.
Cheering the pathway with jubilant songs Of heaven, the home of the soul.
Je-sus and angels and loved ones to see, The toils of our wayfaring o'er.

CHORUS.

Home of the soul, Far a-way land; Free from all sorrow, and sin, and pain,

Sweet it will be in that beau-ti-ful land To meet one an-oth-er a-gain.

80. ONWARD, CHRISTIAN SOLDIERS.

1. Onward, Christian sol-diers, Marching as to war, With the cross of Jesus Going on be-fore. Christ the Ro-yal Mas-ter Leads a-gainst the foe, Forward, in-to bat-tle, See, his banners go.
2. Like a migh-ty ar-my Moves the church of God; Brothers, we are tread-ing Where the saints have trod. We are not di-vi-ded, All one bo-dy we, One in hope and doc-trine, One in cha-ri-ty.

3. Crowns and thrones may perish,
   Kingdoms rise and wane,
   But the church of Jesus
   Constant will remain.
   Gates of hell can never
   'Gainst that church prevail,
   We have Christ's own promise
   Which can never fail.—Cho.

4. Onward, then, ye people,
   Join our happy throng;
   Blend with ours your voices
   In the triumph song.
   Glory, laud, and honor
   Unto Christ the King!
   This through countless ages
   Men and angels sing.—Cho.

ONWARD, CHRISTIAN SOLDIERS.—Concluded.

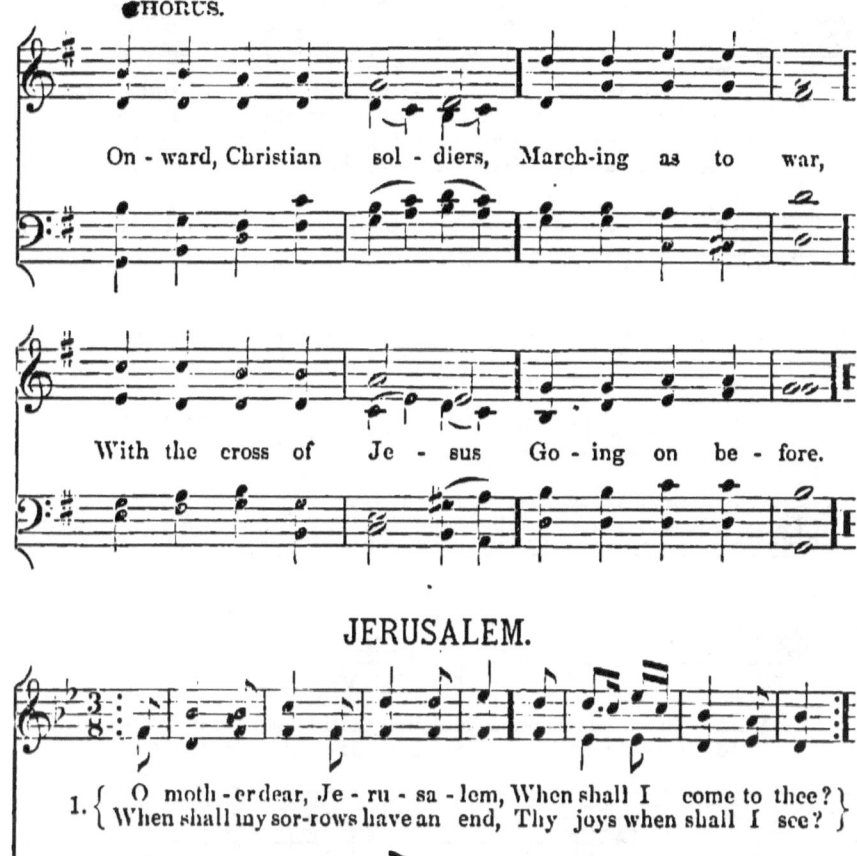

On - ward, Christian sol - diers, March-ing as to war,
With the cross of Je - sus Go - ing on be - fore.

JERUSALEM.

1. { O moth - er dear, Je - ru - sa - lem, When shall I come to thee?
   { When shall my sor-rows have an end, Thy joys when shall I see?

2. O happy harbor of God's saints!
   O sweet and pleasant soil!
   In thee no sorrow can be found,
   Nor grief, nor care, nor toil.

3. Thy walls are made of precious stones,
   Thy bulwarks diamond-square,
   Thy gates are all of orient pearl—
   O God! if I were there!

ALTAR.

1. I lay my sins to Jesus, The spotless Lamb of God;
He bears them all, and frees us From the accursed load.
I bring my guilt to Jesus, To wash my crimson stains
White in his blood most precious, Till not a stain remains.

2. I lay my wants on Jesus, All fullness dwells in him;
He heals all my diseases, He doth my soul redeem:
I lay my griefs on Jesus, My burdens and my cares;
He from them all releases, He all my sorrow shares.

3. I rest my soul on Jesus,
This weary soul of mine;
His right hand me embraces,
I on his breast recline.
I love the name of Jesus,
Immanuel, Christ, the Lord;
Like fragrance on the breezes,
His name abroad is poured.

4. I long to be like Jesus,
Meek, loving, lowly, mild;
I long to be like Jesus,
The Father's holy Child.
I long to be with Jesus
Amid the heavenly throng,
To sing with saints his praises,
To learn the angels' song.

THE PRAYER OF DEVOTION.

1. As down in the sun-less re - treats of the o - cean,
So, deep in my heart the still pray'r of de - vo - tion,
2. As still to the star of its wor - ship, though clouded,
So, dark as I roam, through this win-try world shrouded,

Sweet flow-ers are spring-ing no mor - tal can see;
(Omit) . . . .
The nee - dle points faith-ful - ly o'er the dim sea;
(Omit) . . . .

Un - heard by the world, ri - ses si - lent to thee.
The hope of my spi - rit turns, trembling, to thee.

My God! si - lent to thee! Pure, warm, si - lent to thee!
My God! trembling to thee! True, fond, trembling to thee!

THE BEST FRIEND. 85

1. One there is a-bove all others, Well deserves the name of Friend;
His is love be-yond a brother's, Costly, free, and knows no end.
Which of all our friends, to save us, Could or would have shed his blood?
But our Je-sus died to have us Re-con-ciled in him to God.

2. When he lived on earth abasèd,
  Friend of sinners was his name;
Now, above all glory raised,
  He rejoices in the same.

Oh for grace our hearts to soften!
  Teach us, Lord, at length to love;
We, alas! forget too often
  What a Friend we have above.

I WILL GIVE YOU REST.

1. Come unto me, when shadows darkly ga-ther, When the sad heart is weary and distressed;
2. Large are the mansions in our Father's dwelling, Glad are those homes that sorows never dim;
3. There, like an Eden blossoming in gladness, Bloom the fair flowers by earth so rudely pressed;

Seeking for comfort from your heavenly Father, Come unto me, and I will give you rest.
Sweet are the harps in holy music swelling, Soft are the notes that raise the heav'nly hymn.
Come un-to him, all ye who droop in sadness, "Come un-to me, and I will give you rest."

Tune.—CORONATION.

1. ALL hail the power of Jesus' name!
   Let angels prostrate fall;
   Bring forth the royal diadem,
   And crown him Lord of all.

2. Crown him, ye martyrs of our God,
   Who from his altar call;
   Extol the stem of Jesse's rod,
   And crown him Lord of all.

3. Ye chosen seed of Israel's race,
   Ye ransomed from the fall,
   Hail him who saves you by his grace,
   And crown him Lord of all.

4. Sinners, whose love can ne'er forget
   The wormwood and the gall;
   Go, spread your trophies at his feet,
   And crown him Lord of all.

5. Let every kindred, every tribe,
   On this terrestrial ball,
   To him all majesty ascribe,
   And crown him Lord of all.

GLORY TO JESUS.

1. All glo-ry, laud, and hon-or To thee, Re-deem-er, King!
To whom the lips of chil-dren Made sweet ho-san-nas ring.

2. The com-pa-ny of an-gels Are prais-ing thee on high,
And mor-tal men, and all things Cre-a-ted make re-ply.

CHORUS.
Glo-ry to Jesus, Our gracious King: Glory to Je-sus! We will ev-er sing.

3. The people of the Hebrews,
   With psalms before thee went;
   Our praise and prayer and anthems
   Before thee we present.
   CHORUS.

4. Thou didst accept their praises:
   Accept the prayers we bring,
   Who in all good delightest,
   Thou good and gracious King.
   CHORUS.

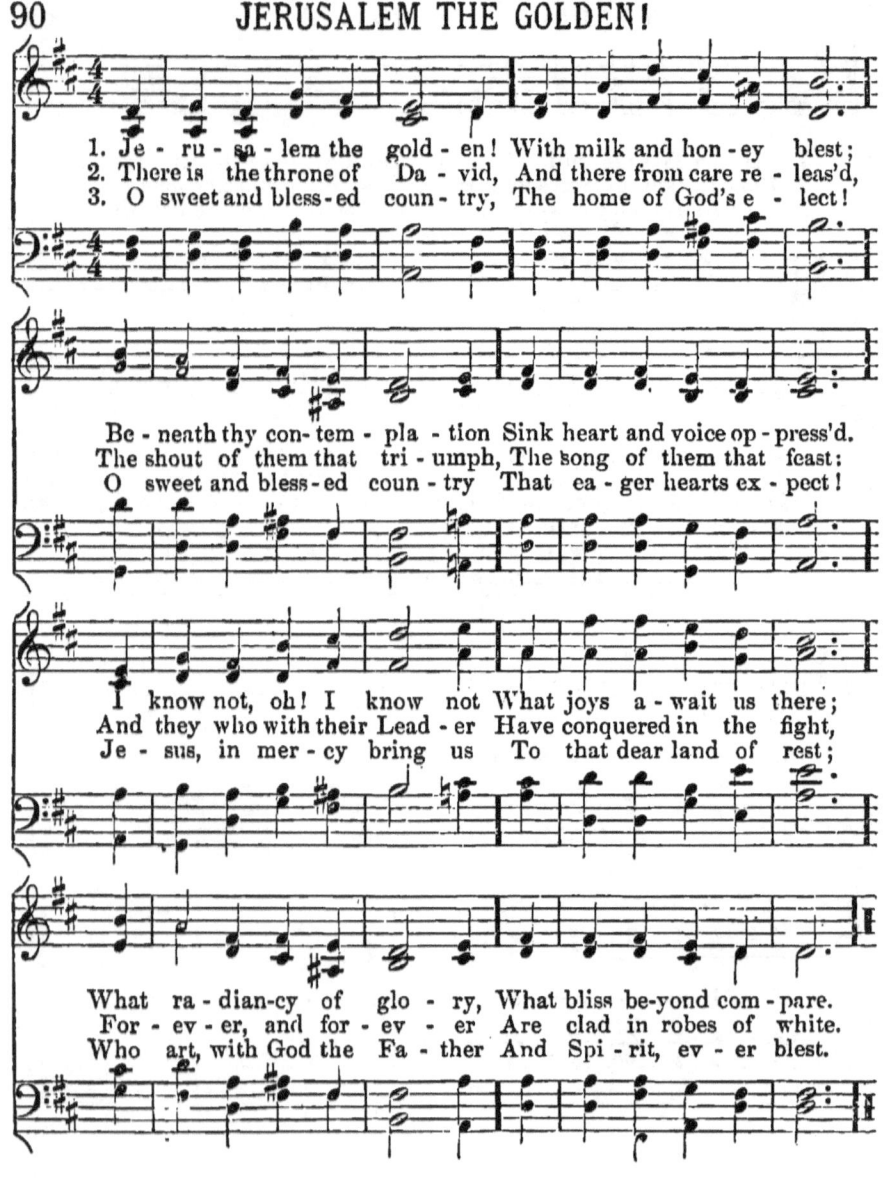

MY SAVIOUR DEAR.

1. My Saviour dear! my Saviour dear! I love to think of thee:

Fain would I sound through all earth's bound Thy matchless love to me.
And all my ways, throughout my days, Shall speak thy love to me:

While I have breath, thy life and death My constant theme shall be.

2. My Saviour dear! my Saviour dear!
I long, I faint to see
Thy lovely face in yon blest place
Thou hast prepared for me.

There, clothed in light, with angels bright,
I'll worship and adore;
And love and praise, through endless days,
A trophy of this power.

92. GUIDE US AND GUARD US.

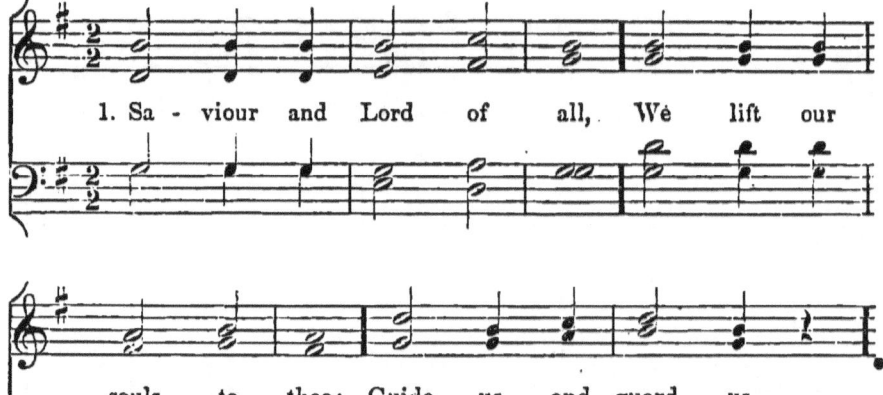

2. When we are full of grief,
   Victims of anxious fear,
   Save us, oh, save us,
   Save us, oh, save us;
   Jesus, then be thou near.

3. Brighten our darkest hours,
   Till the last hour shall come,
   Then, in thy mercy,
   Then, in thy mercy,
   Oh, take thy children home.

4. Saviour and Lord of all,
   How long dost thou delay?
   O gracious Saviour,
   O gracious Saviour,
   Bear us, bear us away.

THE NAME OF JESUS.

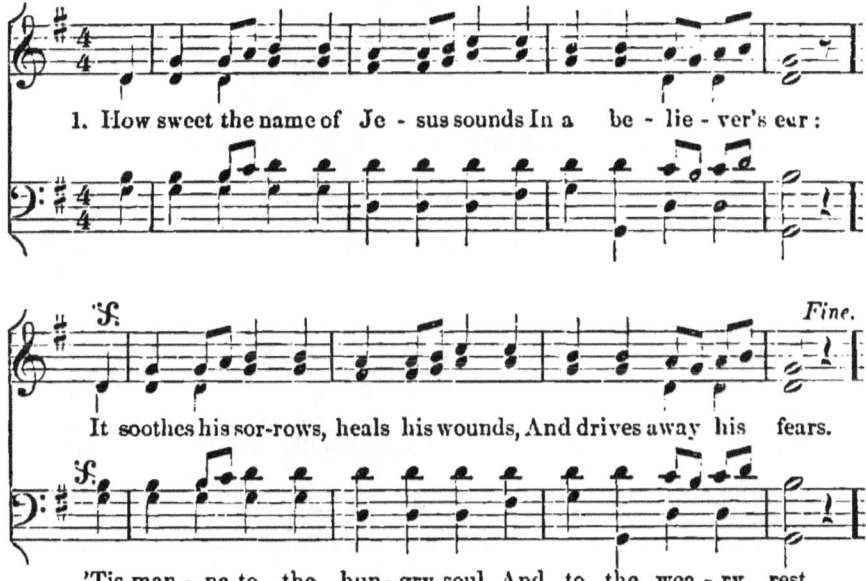

1. How sweet the name of Je-sus sounds In a be-lie-ver's ear:
It soothes his sor-rows, heals his wounds, And drives away his fears.
'Tis man-na to the hun-gry soul, And to the wea-ry rest.
It makes the wounded spi-rit whole, And calms the troubled breast;

2. By thee, my prayers acceptance gain,
   Although with sin defiled;
Satan accuses me in vain,
   And I am owned a child.
Jesus! my Shepherd, Guardian, Friend,
   My Prophet, Priest, and King;
My Lord, my Life, my Way, my End,
   Accept the praise I bring.

3. Weak is the effort of my heart,
   And cold my warmest thought;
But when I see thee as thou art,
   I'll praise thee as I ought.
Till then, I would thy love proclaim,
   With every fleeting breath;
And may the music of thy name,
   Refresh my soul in death.

JESUS IS OUR SHEPHERD.

1. Je-sus is our Shepherd, wiping every tear; Fold-ed in his bo-som, What have we to fear? On-ly let us fol-low whither he doth lead, To the thirs-ty de-sert, or the dew-y mead.

2. Je-sus is our Shepherd, may we know his voice; How its gentle whisper Makes our heart rejoice; Ev-en when he chideth, ten-der is his tone; None but he shall guide us— we are his a-lone.

3. Jesus is our Shepherd,
   For the sheep he bled;
   Every lamb is sprinkled
   With the blood he shed.
   Then on each he places
   His own secret sign;
   "They that have my spirit,
   These," saith he, "are mine."

4. Jesus is our Shepherd,
   Guided by his arm,
   Though the wolves may threaten,
   None can do us harm :
   When we tread death's valley,
   Dark with fearful gloom,
   We will fear no evil,
   Victors o'er the tomb.

2. O Saviour, my Ransom, Redeemer and Friend,
  The life, and the Truth and the Way,
  On thy precious merit alone I depend;
  Dwell in me and keep me, I pray.
  Thy goodness hath opened the door of my heart—
  'Tis open in welcome to thee;
  Come in, blessed Saviour, and never depart;
  Come in, with thy mercy, to me.
          CHORUS.

CHILDREN'S VOICES. 99

3. Now we come, with loving mind,
   Simple faith, and earnest prayer;
Seeking thy dear cross, to find
   Full and free salvation there.
Lamb of God, our Saviour be;
Suffer us to come to thee!

4. Lord, we come! be thou our guide
   Through life's dark and troubled way;
And, when trained and sanctified,
   Raise us to the perfect day.
Then in heaven thy words shall be,
"Suffer them to come to me!"

HOME OF THE BLEST.

1. Oh, when shall I dwell in mansions bright, And Jesus's face behold?
And walk by his side in robes of light, In the streets of shining gold?

CHORUS.
Home of the blest! Mansions of rest! City of God, divine!

2. No pearl from the sea, no gem from the mine,
Can for our sins atone;
We'll trust in the Saviour's love divine,
And cling to his cross alone.
CHORUS.

3. And while we are strangers far from home,
We'll watch, and toil, and pray;
We'll carry the cross, and think of the crown,
And watch for the break of day.
. CHORUS.

HOME OF THE BLEST.—Concluded.

O home of the blest, O mansions of rest! When will ye ev-er be mine?

SPANISH HYMN. 7s.

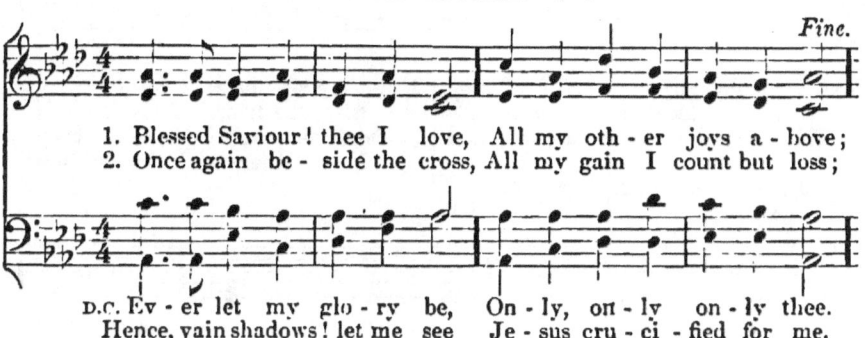

1. Blessed Saviour! thee I love, All my oth-er joys a-bove;
2. Once again be-side the cross, All my gain I count but loss;

D.C. Ev-er let my glo-ry be, On-ly, on-ly on-ly thee.
Hence, vain shadows! let me see Je-sus cru-ci-fied for me.

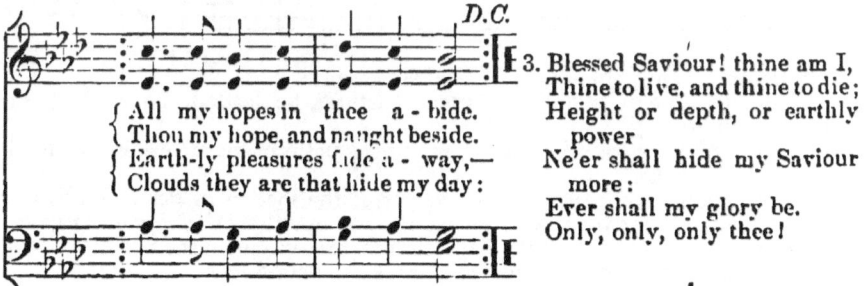

{ All my hopes in thee a-bide.
{ Thou my hope, and naught beside.
{ Earth-ly pleasures fade a-way,—
{ Clouds they are that hide my day:

3. Blessed Saviour! thine am I,
Thine to live, and thine to die;
Height or depth, or earthly power
Ne'er shall hide my Saviour more:
Ever shall my glory be.
Only, only, only thee!

EVENING PRAYER.

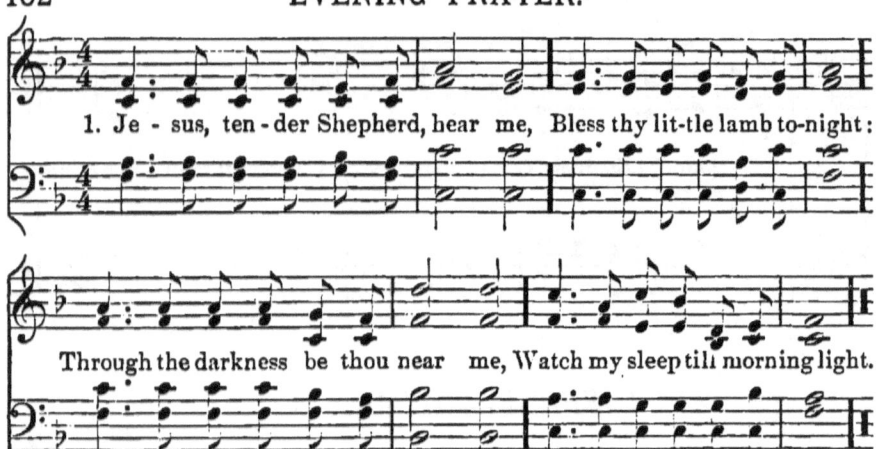

1. Je-sus, ten-der Shepherd, hear me, Bless thy lit-tle lamb to-night: Through the darkness be thou near me, Watch my sleep till morning light.

2. All this day thy hand hath led me,
And I thank thee for thy care;
Thou hast kept, and clothed, and fed me,
Listen to my humble prayer.

3. Let my sins be all forgiven,
Bless the friends I love so well;
Take me, when I die, to heaven,
Happy there with thee to dwell.

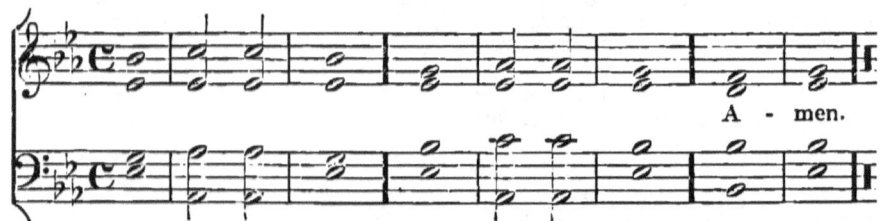

A - men.

1. { The Lord is my Shepherd, I | *shall not want.*
He maketh me to lie down in green pastures, he leadeth me beside the | *still-waters.*

2. { He restoreth my soul, he leadeth me in the paths of righteousness for his | *name's-sake.*
Yea, though I walk through the valley of the shadow of death, I will fear no evil, for thou art with me, thy rod and thy | *staff they comfort me.*

3. { Thou preparest a table before me in the presence of mine enemies: thou anointest my head with oil: my | *cup runneth over.*
Surely goodness and mercy shall follow me all the days of my life: and I will dwell in the house of the | *Lord for ever.* Amen.

ANGELS OF JESUS.

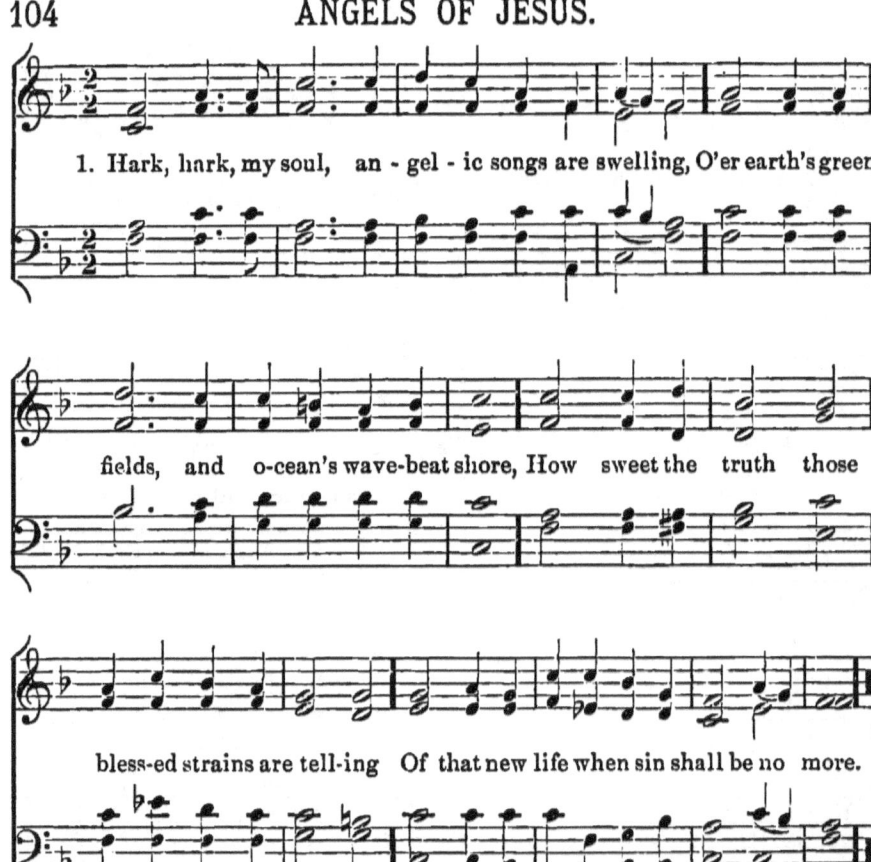

2. Far, far away, like bells at evening pealing,
 The voice of Jesus sounds o'er land and sea,
 And laden souls by thousands meekly stealing,
 Kind Shepherd, turn their weary steps to thee.
   CHORUS.

3. Angels, sing on, your faithful watches keeping;
 Sing us sweet fragments of the songs above;
 Till morning's joy shall end the night of weeping,
 And life's long shadows break in cloudless love.
   CHORUS.

ANGELS OF JESUS. CHORUS.

C. M.

1. The shadows of the evening hours,
   Fall from the darkening sky;
   Upon the fragrance of the flowers
   The dews of evening lie,

2. Before thy throne, O Lord of heaven,
   We kneel at close of day;
   Look on thy children from on high,
   And hear us while we pray.

3. The sorrows of thy servants, Lord,
   Oh, do not thou despise;
   But let the incense of our prayers,
   Before thy mercy rise.

4. The brightness of the coming light,
   Upon the darkness rolls;
   With hopes of future glory chase,
   The shadows on our souls.

5. Let peace, O Lord, thy peace, O God,
   Upon our souls descend;
   From midnight fears and perils, thou
   Our trembling hearts defend.

6. Give us a respite from our toil,
   Calm and subdue our woes;
   Through the long day we suffer, Lord,
   Oh, give us now repose!

106. COME TO ME!

1. Come to me! come to me! All for sin op-pressed; All ye that toil, all ye that mourn, And I will give you rest.
2. Come to me! come to me! Seek my shelter-ing breast; My yoke is sweet, my burd-en light, And I will give you rest.

CHORUS.
We come, we come, to taste thy grace, So full, so rich, so free;

3. Come to me! come to me!
   And ye shall be blest;
   For full of grace and truth am I,
   And I will give you rest.—Cho.

4. Come to me! come to me!
   Jesus cries to me!
   O Saviour dear, thy voice I hear,
   And gladly come to thee.—Cho.

COME TO ME.—Concluded.

Oh thou, the way, the truth, the life! Be-hold, we come to thee.

JESUS, HOLY SAVIOUR.

1. Je-sus, ho-ly Saviour, In thy tender love, Teach us, lit-tle chil-dren, In-to an-gry passions,

To be like the dove: Kind and ve-ry lov-ing To our playmates all, Let us nev-er fall.

2. So that when night cometh
And we kneel to pray,
We may look in gladness
On a well-spent day;

And may feel thy blessing
Fill each little breast,
Like a soft caressing,
As we go to rest.

3. Ev'n for such little ones
    Christ came a child,
   And through this world of sin
    Moved undefiled.
   Oh, for his sake, I pray,
   Lead them, my God, to thee,
    Lead them, &c.

4. Yea, though my faith be dim,
    I would believe
   That thou, this precious gift
    Wilt now receive.
   Oh, take their young hearts now,
   Lead them, my God, to thee,
    Lead them, &c.

STRANGERS AND PILGRIMS.

1. This life so brief, is full of grief, Earth is a home of sor-row;
2. Life's troubled stream glides like a dream, Thro' sun and shadow flowing;
3. And so would we, as pilgrims be, And live on earth as strangers;

Nor can we know, as on we go, What shall be-fall to-mor-row.
It rolls a-long with current strong, Onward for-ev-er go-ing.
So, day by day, pur-sue our way, Thro' snares, and toils, and dangers.

CHORUS.

Chil-dren of dust, we put our trust In him who can de-li-ver;
And seek our rest a-mong the blest, Be-yond the gloomy riv-er.

THE SUNDAY-SCHOOL ARMY.

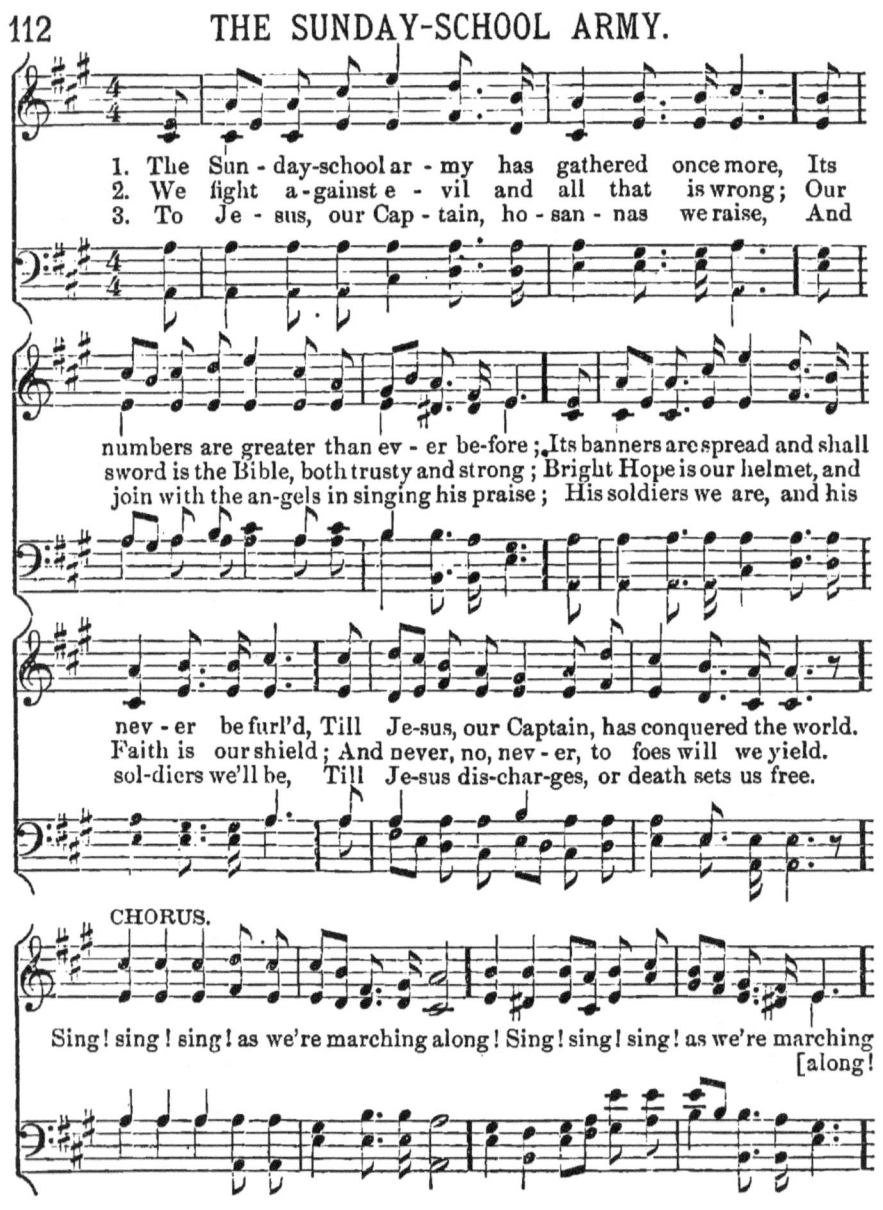

1. The Sunday-school army has gathered once more, Its numbers are greater than ever before; Its banners are spread and shall never be furl'd, Till Jesus, our Captain, has conquered the world.
2. We fight against evil and all that is wrong; Our sword is the Bible, both trusty and strong; Bright Hope is our helmet, and Faith is our shield; And never, no, never, to foes will we yield.
3. To Jesus, our Captain, hosannas we raise, And join with the angels in singing his praise; His soldiers we are, and his soldiers we'll be, Till Jesus discharges, or death sets us free.

CHORUS.
Sing! sing! sing! as we're marching along! Sing! sing! sing! as we're marching [along!

THE SUNDAY-SCHOOL ARMY.—Concluded.

Our ar-my is no-ble, And our Lea-der is strong,

And with a cheer-ful song we go march-ing a-long.

Tune.—BETHANY.

1. NEARER, my God, to thee,
   Nearer to thee:
   Ev'n though it be a cross
   That raiseth me,
   Still all my song shall be,
   Nearer, my God, to thee,
   Nearer to thee.

2. Though like a wanderer,
   Daylight all gone,
   Darkness be over me,
   My rest a stone,
   Yet in my dreams I'd be
   Nearer, my God, to thee,
   Nearer to thee.

3. There let the way appear
   Steps up to heaven;
   All that thou sendest me
   In mercy given,
   Angels to beckon me
   Nearer, my God, to thee,
   Nearer to thee.

4. Then with my waking thoughts,
   Bright with thy praise,
   Out of my stony griefs,
   Bethel I'll raise;
   So by my woes to be
   Nearer, my God, to thee,
   Nearer to thee.

114. THE SAVIOUR'S LEGACY.

1. Our blest Re-deem-er, ere he breath'd His ten-der, last fare-well,
2. He came sweet influence to im-part, A gra-cious, will-ing Guest,
3. And his that gen-tle voice we hear, Soft as the breath of ev'n,

A guide, a com-for-ter, bequeathed With us to dwell.
While he can find one hum-ble heart Where-in to rest.
That checks each thought, that calms each fear And speaks of heav'n.

4. And every virtue we possess,
   And every conquest won,
   And every thought of holiness,
   Are his alone.

5. Spirit of purity and grace,
   Our weakness, pitying, see;
   Oh, make our hearts thy dwelling-place,
   And worthier thee!

---

1. Our life is but a fading dawn,
   Its noon how quickly past;
   Lead us, O Christ, when all is gone,
   Safe home at last.

2. Oh, by thy soul-inspiring grace
   Uplift our hearts on high;
   Help us to look to that bright place
   Beyond the sky:

3. Where light, and love, and joy, and peace,
   All undivided reign;
   And thronging angels never cease,
   Their deathless strain:

4. Where saints are clothed in spotless white,
   And shadows never fall;
   When thou, eternal light of light,
   Art Lord of all.

DAWN.

1. Oh, cease, my wand'ring soul, On rest-less wing to roam;
2. Be-hold the ark of God! Be-hold the o-pen door!
3. There, safe thou shalt a-bide, There sweet shall be thy rest,

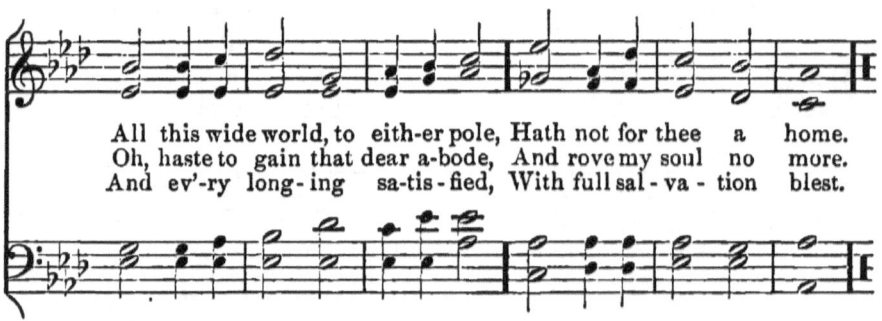

All this wide world, to eith-er pole, Hath not for thee a home.
Oh, haste to gain that dear a-bode, And rove my soul no more.
And ev'-ry long-ing sa-tis-fied, With full sal-va-tion blest.

1. One sweetly solemn thought
   Comes to me o'er and o'er,—
   Nearer my home to-day, am I
   Than e'er I've been before;

2. Nearer my Father's house,
   Where many mansions be;
   Nearer my Saviour's glorious
      throne;
   Nearer the crystal sea;

3. Nearer the bound of life,
   Where burdens are laid down;
   Nearer to leave the heavy cross;
   Nearer to gain the crown.

4. But, lying dark between,
   Winding down through the night
   There rolls the deep and unknown
      stream
   That leads at last to light.

5. E'en now, perchance, my feet
   Are slipping on the brink,
   And I, to-day, am nearer home,—
   Nearer than now I think.

6. Father, perfect my trust!
   Strengthen my power of faith!
   Nor let me stand, at last, alone
   Upon the shore of death.

BOYLSTON.

1. Not all the blood of beasts,
   On Jewish altars slain,
   Could give the guilty conscience peace,
   Or wash away the stain.

2. But Christ, the heavenly Lamb,
   Takes all our sins away,—
   A sacrifice of nobler name,
   And richer blood than they.

3. My faith would lay her hand
   On that dear head of thine,
   While like a penitent I stand,
   And there confess my sin.

4. My soul looks back to see
   The burdens thou didst bear,
   When hanging on th' accursèd tree,
   And hopes her guilt was there.

OLMUTZ.

1. I love thy kingdom, Lord,—
   The house of thine abode,
   The Church our blest Redeemer saved
   With his own precious blood.

2. I love thy Church, O God!
   Her walls before thee stand,
   Dear as the apple of thine eye,
   And graven on thy hand.

3. For her my tears shall fall,
   For her my prayers ascend;
   To her my cares and toils be given,
   Till toils and cares shall end.

ST. THOMAS.

1. Come, Holy Spirit, come!
   Let thy bright beams arise;
   Dispel the sorrow from our minds,
   The darkness from our eyes.

2. Convince us of our sin;
   Then lead to Jesus' blood,
   And to our wondering view reveal
   The secret love of God.

3. Revive our drooping faith,
   Our doubts and fears remove,
   And kindle in our breasts the flame
   Of never-dying love.

4. 'Tis thine to cleanse the heart,
   To sanctify the soul,
   To pour fresh life in every part,
   And new-create the whole.

5. Dwell, Spirit, in our hearts;
   Our minds from bondage free;
   Then shall we know, and praise, and love
   The Father, Son, and thee.

BOYLSTON.

1. Blest are the sons of peace
   Whose hearts and hopes are one;
   Whose kind designs to serve and please
   Through all their actions run.

2. Blest is the pious house
   Where zeal and friendship meet:
   Their songs of praise, their mingled vows
   Make their communion sweet.

3. From those celestial springs
   Such streams of pleasure flow,
   As no increase of riches brings,
   Nor honors can bestow.

4. Thus on the heavenly hills
   The saints are blest above,
   Where joy, like morning-dew distils,
   And all the air is love!

STOCKWELL. 8s & 7s.

1. Always with us, always with us,—Words of cheer and words of love;
2. With us when we toil in sad-ness, Sowing much and reaping none;

Thus the ri-sen Saviour whispers, From his dwelling-place a-bove.
Tell-ing us that in the fu-ture Gold-en harvests shall be won.

3. With us when the storm is sweeping
    O'er our pathway dark and drear;
   Waking hope within our bosoms,
    Stilling every anxious fear.

4. With us in the lonely valley,
    When we cross the chilling stream;
   Lighting up the steps to glory
    With salvation's radiant beam.

---

1. GENTLY, Lord, oh, gently lead us
    Through this lonely vale of tears;
   Through the changes thou'st decreed us,
    Till our last, great change appears.

2. When temptation's darts assail us,
    When in devious paths we stray,
   Let thy goodness never fail us,
    Lead us in thy perfect way.

3. In the hour of pain and anguish,
    In the hour when death draws near,
   Suffer not our hearts to languish,
    Suffer not our souls to fear.

4. And, when mortal life is ended,
    Bid us on thy bosom rest,
   Till, by angel-bands attended,
    We awake among the blest.

WILMOT.

1. In the cross of Christ I glory,
    Towering o'er the wrecks of time;
   All the light of sacred story
    Gathers round its head sublime.

2. When the woes of life o'ertake me,
    Hopes deceive, and fears annoy,
   Never shall the cross forsake me:
    Lo! it glows with peace and joy.

3. When the sun of bliss is beaming
    Light and love upon my way,
   From the cross the radiance streaming,
    Adds new lustre to the day.

4. Bane and blessing, pain and pleasure,
    By the cross are sanctified;
   Peace is there, that knows no measure,
    Joys that through all time abide.

SOUTH CHURCH.

1. Take my heart, O Father, take it!
    Make and keep it all thine own;
   Let thy Spirit melt and break it—
    This proud heart of sin and stone.

2. Father, make it pure and lowly,
    Fond of peace, and far from strife;
   Turning from the paths unholy
    Of this vain and sinful life.

3. Ever let thy grace surround it;
    Strengthen it with power divine,
   Till thy cords of love have bound it:
    Make it to be wholly thine.

NUREMBURG.

1. Gracious Spirit, Love divine!
    Let thy light within me shine;
   All my guilty fears remove,
    Fill me with thy heavenly love.

2. Speak thy pardoning grace to me,
    Set the burdened sinner free;
   Lead me to the Lamb of God,
    Wash me in his precious blood.

3. Life and peace to me impart,
    Seal salvation on my heart;
   Breathe thyself into my breast,—
    Earnest of immortal rest.

4. Let me never from thee stray,
    Keep me in the narrow way;
   Fill my soul with joy divine,
    Keep me, Lord! forever thine.

PLEYEL'S HYMN. 7s.

1. O my Saviour, guardian true,
    All my life is thine to keep;
   At thy feet my work I do,
    In thine arms I fall asleep.

2. Leaning on thy tender care,
    Thou hast led my soul aright;
   Fervent was my morning prayer;
    Joyful is my song to-night.

3. Tender mercies on my way
    Falling softly like the dew,
   Sent me freshly every day—
    I will bless the Lord for you.

4. Source of all that comforts me,
    Well of joy for which I long;
   Let the song I sing to thee,
    Be an everlasting song!

120 KEBLE. L. M.

1. Sun of my soul! thou Saviour dear, It is not night if thou be near: Oh, may no earth-born cloud arise To hide thee from thy servant's eyes!
2. When soft the dews of kindly sleep My weary eyelids gently steep, Be my last thought,—how sweet to rest Forever on my Saviour's breast!
3. Be near to bless me when I wake, Ere through the world my way I take; Till in the ocean of thy love I lose myself in heav'n above.

1. When I survey the wondrous cross
On which the Prince of glory died,
My richest gain I count but loss,
And pour contempt on all my pride.

2. Forbid it, Lord, that I should boast,
Save in the death of Christ my God,
All the vain things that charm me most,
I sacrifice them to his blood.

3. See, from his head, his hands, his feet,
Sorrow and love flow mingled down:
Did e'er such love and sorrow meet,
Or thorns compose so rich a crown?

4. Were the whole realm of nature mine,
That were a present far too small;
Love so amazing, so divine,
Demands my soul, my life, my all.

KEBLE.

1. With tearful eyes I look around,
   Life seems a dark and stormy sea;
   Yet, 'midst the gloom, I hear a sound,
   A heavenly whisper, "Come to me."

2. It tells me of a place of rest—
   It tells me where my soul may flee;
   Oh, to the weary, faint, oppressed,
   How sweet the bidding, "Come to me."

3. When nature shudders, loath to part
   From all I love, enjoy, and see;
   When a faint chill steals o'er my heart,
   A sweet voice utters, "Come to me."

3. Come, for all else must fail and die;
   Earth is no resting-place for thee;
   Heavenward direct thy weeping eye;
   I am thy portion, "Come to me."

4. Oh, voice of mercy! voice of love!
   In conflict, grief, and agony,
   Support me, cheer me from above!
   And gently whisper, "Come to me."

OLD HUNDRED.

1. Worthy the Lamb of boundless sway,
   In earth and heaven the Lord of all:
   Let all the powers of earth obey,
   And low before his footstool fall.

2. Higher, still higher, swell the strain;
   Creation's voice the note prolong!
   Jesus, the Lamb, shall ever reign:
   Let hallelujahs crown the song!

HAMBURG.

1. Just as I am, without one plea,
   But that thy blood was shed for me,
   And that thou bid'st me come to thee,
   O Lamb of God, I come! I come!

2. Just as I am, and waiting not
   To rid my soul of one dark blot,
   To thee, whose blood can cleanse each spot,
   O Lamb of God, I come! I come!

3. Just as I am, thou wilt receive,
   Wilt welcome, pardon, cleanse, relieve;
   Because thy promise I believe,
   O Lamb of God, I come! I come!

4. Just as I am, thy love unknown
   Hath broken every barrier down;
   Now, to be thine, yea, thine alone,
   O Lamb of God, I come! I come!

ROCKINGHAM.

1. How sweet to leave the world awhile,
   And seek the presence of our Lord!
   Dear Saviour! on thy people smile,
   And come, according to thy word.

2. From busy scenes we now retreat,
   That we may here converse with thee:
   Ah! Lord, behold us at thy feet;—
   Let this the "gate of heaven" be.

3. "Chief of ten thousand!" now appear,
   That we by faith may see thy face:
   Oh! speak, that we thy voice may hear,
   And let thy presence fill this place.

122 INVITATION. C. M.

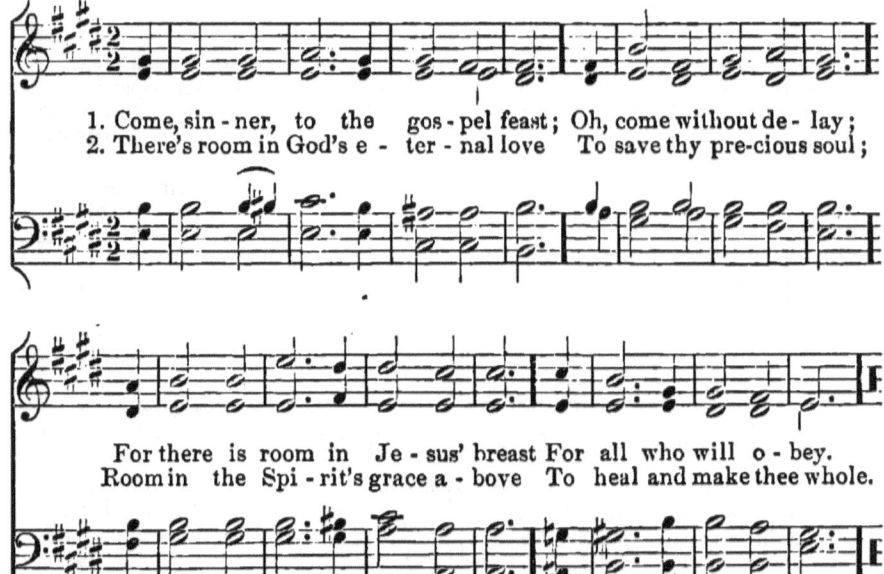

1. Come, sinner, to the gospel feast; Oh, come without delay;
For there is room in Jesus' breast For all who will obey.

2. There's room in God's eternal love To save thy precious soul;
Room in the Spirit's grace above To heal and make thee whole.

3. There's room within the church, redeemed
With blood of Christ divine;
Room in the white-robed throng convened,
For that dear soul of thine.

4. There's room around thy Father's board
For thee and thousands more:
Oh, come and welcome to the Lord;
Yea, come this very hour.

---

1. I LOVE to steal awhile away
From every cumbering care,
And spend the hours of setting day
In humble, grateful prayer.

2. I love, in solitude, to shed,
The penitential tear;
And all his promises to plead,
Where none but God can hear.

3. I love to think on mercies past,
And future good implore;
And all my cares and sorrows cast
On him whom I adore.

4. I love, by faith, to take a view
Of brighter scenes in heaven;
The prospect doth my strength renew,
While here by tempests driven.

ARLINGTON.

1. Thou dear Redeemer, dying Lamb,
   I love to hear of thee;
   No music's like thy charming name,
   Nor half so sweet can be.

2. Oh, may I ever hear thy voice
   In mercy to me speak;
   In thee, my Priest, will I rejoice,
   And thy salvation seek.

3. My Jesus shall be still my theme,
   While on this earth I stay;
   I'll sing my Jesus' lovely name,
   When all things else decay.

4. When I appear in yonder cloud,
   With all his favored throng,
   Then will I sing more sweet, more loud,
   And Christ shall be my song.

MARLOW.

1. Come, Holy Spirit, heavenly Dove!
   With all thy quickening powers;
   Kindle a flame of sacred love
   In these cold hearts of ours.

2. Look, how we grovel here below,
   Fond of these trifling toys;
   Our souls can neither fly nor go
   To reach eternal joys.

3. In vain we tune our formal songs,
   In vain we strive to rise;
   Hosannas languish on our tongues,
   And our devotion dies.

4. Dear Lord! and shall we ever live
   At this poor dying rate?
   Our love so faint, so cold to thee,
   And thine to us so great?

5. Come, Holy Spirit, heavenly Dove,
   With all thy quickening powers;
   Come, shed abroad a Saviour's love,
   And that shall kindle ours.

BALERMA.

1. Oh for a closer walk with God,
   A calm and heavenly frame,
   A light to shine upon the road
   That leads me to the Lamb!

2. Return, O holy Dove! return,
   Sweet Messenger of rest!
   I hate the sins that made thee mourn,
   And drove thee from my breast.

3. The dearest idol I have known,
   Whate'er that idol be,
   Help me to tear it from thy throne,
   And worship only thee.

4. So shall my walk be close with God,
   Calm and serene my frame;
   So purer light shall mark the road
   That leads me to the Lamb.

DEDHAM.

1. Oh, what a lonely path were ours,
   Could we, O Father, see
   No home of rest beyond it all,
   No guide, no help in thee!

2. But thou art near and with us still,
   To guide us in the way
   That leads along this vale of tears
   To the bright realms of day.

3. There shall thy glory, O our God,
   Break fully on our view,
   And we, thy saints, rejoice to find
   That all thy word was true.

124   CALM. S. M.

1. My spirit on thy care, Blest Saviour I recline;
Thou wilt not leave me to despair, For thou art love divine.

2. In thee I place my trust; On thee I calmly rest:
I know thee good, I know thee just, And count thy choice the best.

3. Whatev'er events betide,
   Thy will they all perform;
Safe in thy breast my head I hide,
   Nor fear the coming storm.

4. Let good or ill befall,
   It must be good for me,—
Secure of having thee in all,
   Of having all in thee.

---

1. For all thy saints, O God,
   Who strove in Christ to live,
Who followed him, obeyed, adored,
   Our grateful hymn receive.

2. For all thy saints, O God,
   Accept our thankful cry,
Who counted Christ their great reward
   And yearned for him to die.

3. They all, in life and death,
   With him, their Lord, in view,
Learned from thy Holy Spirit's breath
   To suffer and to do.

4. For this thy name we bless,
   And humbly pray that we
May follow them in holiness,
   And live and die in thee.

FEDERAL STREET. L. M. 125

1. O love divine! that stooped to share Our sharpest pang, our bitterest tear,
2. Though long the weary way we tread, And sorrow crown each lingering year,

On thee we cast each earth-born care, We smile at pain while thou art near.
No path we shun, no dark-ness dread, Our hearts still whispering thou art near.

3. When drooping pleasure turns to grief,
And trembling faith is changed to fear,
The murmuring wind, the quivering leaf,
Shall softly tell us thou art near.

4. On thee we fling our burdening woe,
O Love divine, forever dear;
Content to suffer while we know,
Living or dying, thou art near!

---

1. JESUS! and shall it ever be,
A mortal man ashamed of thee?—
Ashamed of thee whom angels praise,
Whose glories shine through endless days.

2. Ashamed of Jesus! sooner far
Let evening blush to own a star;
He sheds the beams of light divine
O'er this benighted soul of mine.

3. Ashamed of Jesus! that dear Friend
On whom my hopes of heaven depend!
No;— when I blush, be this my shame,
That I no more revere his name.

4. Ashamed of Jesus! yes, I may,
When I've no guilt to wash away;
No tear to wipe, no good to crave,
No fears to quell, no soul to save.

MANOAH. C. M.

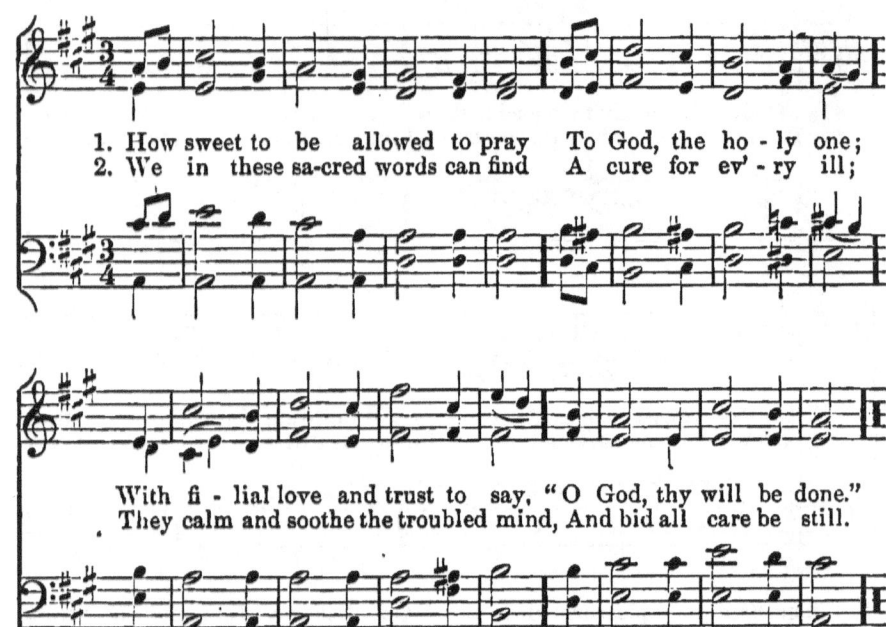

1. How sweet to be allowed to pray To God, the ho-ly one;
2. We in these sa-cred words can find A cure for ev'-ry ill;

With fi-lial love and trust to say, "O God, thy will be done."
They calm and soothe the troubled mind, And bid all care be still.

3. Oh, let that will which gave me breath,
And an immortal soul,
In joy, in grief, in life or death,
My every wish control.

4. Oh, could my heart thus ever pray,
Thus imitate thy Son!
Teach me, O God, with truth to say,
"Thy will, not mine, be done."

---

1. To whom, my Saviour, shall I go,
If I depart from thee?
My guide through all this vale of woe,
And more than all to me.

2. The world reject thy gentle reign,
And pay thy death with scorn;
Oh! they could plait thy crown again,
And sharpen every thorn.

3. But I have felt thy dying love
Breathe gently through my heart,
To whisper hope of joys above,—
And can we ever part?

4. Ah! no, with thee I'll walk below,
My journey to the grave:
To whom, my Saviour, shall I go,
When only thou canst save?

COWPER.

1. THERE is a fountain filled with blood,
    Drawn from Immanuel's veins;
    And sinners, plunged beneath that flood,
    Lose all their guilty stains.

2. The dying thief rejoiced to see
    That fountain in his day;
    And there may I, though vile as he,
    Wash all my sins away.

3. Dear dying Lamb, thy precious blood
    Shall never lose its power,
    Till all the ransomed church of God
    Be saved, to sin no more.

4. E'er since, by faith, I saw the stream
    Thy flowing wounds supply,
    Redeeming love has been my theme,
    And shall be till I die.

NAOMI.

1. FATHER! whate'er of earthly bliss
    Thy sovereign will denies,
    Accepted at thy throne of grace,
    Let this petition rise:—

2. "Give me a calm, a thankful heart,
    From every murmur free!
    The blessings of thy grace impart,
    And make me live to thee.

3. "Let the sweet hope that thou art mine,
    My life and death attend;
    Thy presence through my journey shine,
    And crown my journey's end."

WOODSTOCK.

1. THE roseate hues of early dawn,
    The brightness of the day,
    The crimson of the sunset sky,
    How fast they fade away!

2. Oh for the pearly gates of heaven,
    Oh for the golden floor,
    Oh for the Sun of righteousness,
    That setteth nevermore!

3. Oh for a heart that never sins,
    Oh for a soul washed white,
    Oh for a voice to praise our King,
    Nor weary, day nor night!

4. Here faith is ours, and heavenly hope,
    And grace to lead us higher;
    But there are perfectness and peace,
    Beyond our best desire.

5. Oh, by thy love and anguish, Lord,
    And by thy life laid down,
    Grant that we fall not from thy grace,
    Nor cast away our crown.

MANOAH.

1. THERE is an hour of hallowed peace,
    For those with cares oppressed,
    When sighs and sorrowing tears shall cease,
    And all be hushed to rest.

2. 'Tis then the soul is freed from fears
    And doubts which here annoy;
    Then they who oft have sown in tears
    Shall reap again in joy.

3. There is a home of sweet repose,
    Where storms assail no more;
    The stream of endless pleasure flows
    On that celestial shore.

128. SOUTH CHURCH. 8s & 7s.

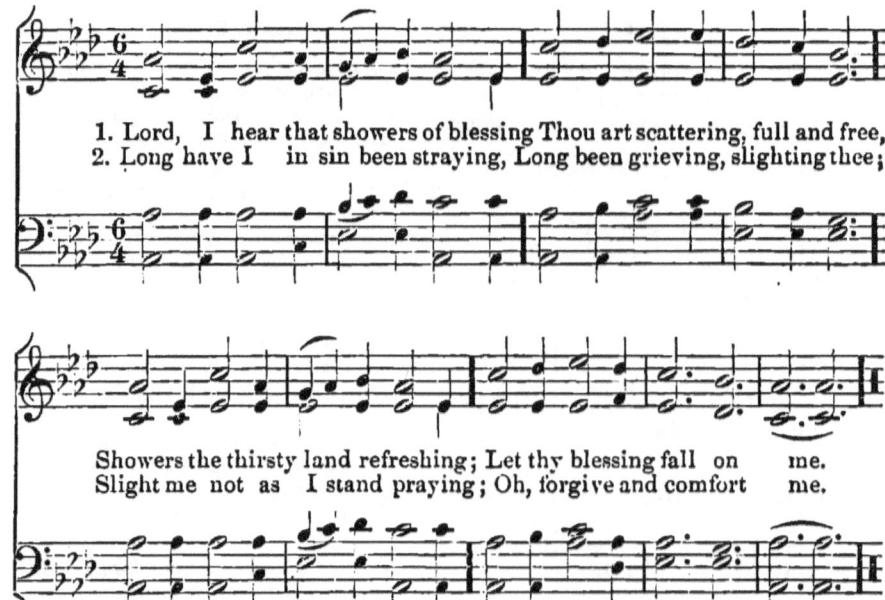

1. Lord, I hear that showers of blessing Thou art scattering, full and free,
Showers the thirsty land refreshing; Let thy blessing fall on me.

2. Long have I in sin been straying, Long been grieving, slighting thee;
Slight me not as I stand praying; Oh, forgive and comfort me.

3. Pass me not, O gracious Saviour,
Sinful though my heart may be;
Give me tokens of thy favor,
Speak some word of grace to me.

4. Pass me not; thy lost one bringing,
Bind my heart, O Lord, to thee:
While the streams of life are springing,
Blessing others, oh, bless me!

---

1. Come, thou Fount of every blessing,
Tune my heart to sing thy grace;
Streams of mercy, never ceasing,
Call for songs of loudest praise.

2. Jesus sought me when a stranger,
Wandering from the fold of God;
He, to save my soul from danger,
Interposed his precious blood.

3. Oh, to grace how great a debtor
Daily I'm constrained to be;
Let that grace, Lord, like a fetter,
Bind my wandering soul to thee.

4. Prone to wander, Lord, I feel it,
Prone to leave the God I love;
Here's my heart! oh take and seal it,
Seal it from thy courts above.

OLIVET.

1. My faith looks up to thee,
    Thou Lamb of Calvary,
      Saviour divine!
    Now hear me while I pray;
    Take all my guilt away;
      Oh, let me, from this day,
      Be wholly thine!

2. May thy rich grace impart
    Strength to my fainting heart;
      My zeal inspire;
    As thou hast died for me,
    Oh! may my love to thee
    Pure, warm, and changeless be—
      A living fire.

3. While life's dark maze I tread,
    And griefs around me spread,
      Be thou my guide;
    Bid darkness turn to day,
    Wipe sorrow's tears away;
      Nor let me ever stray
      From thee aside.

4. When ends life's transient dream,
    When death's cold, sullen stream
      Shall o'er me roll:
    Blest Saviour, then, in love,
    Fear and distrust remove;
      Oh, bear me safe above—
      A ransomed soul.

ROCK OF AGES.

1. Rock of Ages! cleft for me;
    Let me hide myself in thee!
    Let the water and the blood,
    From thy riven side that flowed,
    Be of sin the double cure,—
    Cleanse me from its guilt and power.

2. Could my zeal no respite know,
    Could my tears forever flow,
    All for sin could not atone:
    Thou must save, and thou alone!
    Nothing in my hand I bring;
    Simply to thy cross I cling.

3. While I draw this fleeting breath,
    When my eyelids close in death,
    When I soar to worlds unknown,
    See thee on thy judgment throne,—
    Rock of Ages! cleft for me,
    Let me hide myself in thee!

SOUTH CHURCH.

1. Light of those whose dreary dwelling
    Borders on the shades of death,
    Rise on us, thyself revealing,—
    Rise, and chase the clouds beneath.

2. Thou of heaven and earth Creator,
    In our deepest darkness rise;
    Scatter all the night of nature;
    Pour the day upon our eyes.

3. Still we wait for thine appearing;
    Life and joy thy beams impart,
    Chasing all our fears, and cheering
    Every poor, benighted heart.

4. By thine all-sufficient merit,
    Every burdened soul release;
    Every weary, wandering spirit
    Guide into thy perfect peace.

ASPIRATION. S. M.

1. My Saviour bids me come; Ah! why do I de-lay?
   He calls the wea-ry sin-ner home, And yet from him I stay!

2. What worldly tie must break? What i-dol yet de-part,
   Which will not let the Saviour take Pos-ses-sion of my heart?

3. Jesus, the hind'rance show
   Which I have feared to see;
   And let me now consent to know
   What keeps me back from thee.

4. Oh! break the fatal chain,
   And all my bonds remove;
   Nor let one bosom-sin remain,
   To keep me from thy love.

---

1. The Comforter has come;
   We feel his presence here;
   Our hearts would now no longer roam,
   But bow in filial fear.

2. This tenderness of love,
   This hush of solemn power,—
   'Tis heaven descending from above,
   To fill this favored hour.

3. Earth's darkness all has fled,
   Heaven's light serenely shines,
   And every heart divinely led,
   To holy thought inclines.

4. No more let sin deceive,
   Nor earthly cares betray,
   Oh, let us never, never grieve
   The Comforter away!

ST. THOMAS.

1. Come, kingdom of our God,
   Sweet reign of light and love!
   Shed peace, and hope, and joy, abroad,
   And wisdom from above.

2. Over our spirits first
   Extend thy healing reign;
   There raise and quench the sacred thirst
   That never pains again.

3. Come, kingdom of our God!
   And make the broad earth thine:
   Stretch o'er her lands and isles the rod
   That flowers with grace divine.

4. Soon may all tribes be blest
   With fruit from life's glad tree;
   And in its shade like brothers rest,
   Sons of one family.

DAWN.

1. The Spirit, in our hearts,
   Is whispering, "Sinner, come;"
   The Bride, the Church of Christ, proclaims
   To all his children, "Come!"

2. Let him that heareth say
   To all about him, "Come!"
   Let him that thirsts for righteousness,
   To Christ, the fountain, come!

3. Yes, whosoever will.
   Oh, let him freely come,
   And freely drink the stream of life;
   'Tis Jesus bids him come.

4. Lo! Jesus, who invites,
   Declares, "I quickly come;"
   Lord, even so! we wait thine hour;
   O blest Redeemer, come!

ASPIRATION.

1. Oh what, if we are Christ's,
   Is earthly shame or loss?
   Bright shall the crown of glory be,
   When we have borne the cross.

2. Keen was the trial once,
   Bitter the cup of woe,
   When martyred saints, baptized in blood,
   Christ's sufferings shared below.

3. Bright is their glory now,
   Boundless their joy above,
   Where, on the bosom of their God,
   They rest in perfect love.

4. Lord, may that grace be ours,
   Like them in faith to bear
   All that of sorrow, grief, or pain
   May be our portion here.

DENNIS.

1. How gentle God's commands!
   How kind his precepts are!
   Come, cast your burdens on the Lord,
   And trust his constant care.

2. Beneath his watchful eye
   His saints securely dwell;
   That hand which bears all nature up,
   Shall guard his children well.

3. Why should this anxious load
   Press down your weary mind?
   Haste to your heavenly Father's throne,
   And sweet refreshment find.

4. His goodness stands approved,
   Unchanged from day to day:
   I'll drop my burden at his feet,
   And bear a song away.

132. REST.

1. There is a bless-ed home Be-yond this land of woe, Where tri-als nev-er come, Nor tears of sor-row flow;
2. Where faith is lost in sight, And pa-tient hope is crowned, And ev-er-last-ing light Its glo-ry throws a-round.

3. There is a land of peace;
   Good angels know it well;
   Glad songs that never cease
   Within its portals swell.

4. Look up, ye saints of God!
   Nor fear to tread below
   The path your Saviour trod,
   Of daily toil and woe.

---

1. My Jesus, as thou wilt
   Oh, may thy will be mine!
   Into thy hand of love
   I would my all resign.

2. Through sorrow or through joy,
   Conduct me as thine own,
   And help me still to say,
   My Lord, thy will be done!

3. My Jesus, as thou wilt!
   Though seen through many a tear,
   Let not my star of hope
   Grow dim or disappear.

4. Thou, Lord, on earth along
   The thorny path hast gone;
   Then lead me after thee;—
   My Lord, thy will be done!

5. My Jesus, as thou wilt!
   When death itself draws nigh,
   To thy dear wounded side
   I would for refuge fly.

DEAR JESUS.

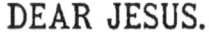

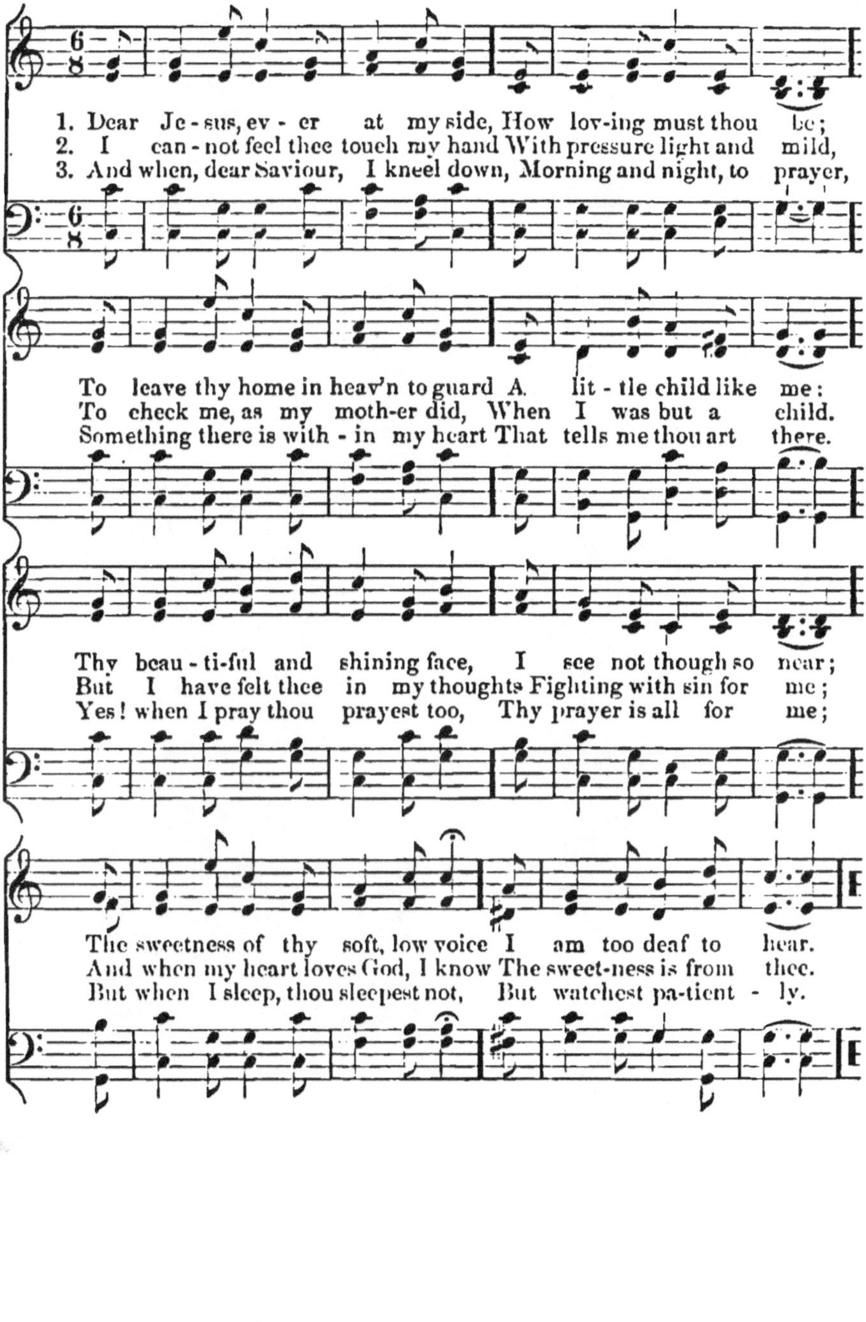
1. Dear Je - sus, ev - er at my side, How lov-ing must thou be;
2. I can - not feel thee touch my hand With pressure light and mild,
3. And when, dear Saviour, I kneel down, Morning and night, to prayer,
To leave thy home in heav'n to guard A lit - tle child like me:
To check me, as my moth-er did, When I was but a child.
Something there is with - in my heart That tells me thou art there.
Thy beau - ti-ful and shining face, I see not though so near;
But I have felt thee in my thoughts Fighting with sin for me;
Yes! when I pray thou prayest too, Thy prayer is all for me;
The sweetness of thy soft, low voice I am too deaf to hear.
And when my heart loves God, I know The sweet-ness is from thee.
But when I sleep, thou sleepest not, But watchest pa-tient - ly.

INDEX OF TUNES.

	PAGE
A Lamp to my Feet.....*L. O. Emerson*	110
Above the Bright Blue Sky, *Rev. E. P. Parker*	38
Altar.....................*Asa Hull*	82
Angels of Jesus................*Arranged*	104
Art Thou Weary..*Rev. E. P. Parker*	60
Aspiration............*Rev. E. P. Parker*	130
At the Door................*J. E. Gould*	98
Beautiful Land of Rest, *Rev. E. P. Parker*	62
Beautiful River.........*Rev. R. Lowry*	109
Brightest and Best................*Mozart*	19
Brightly Gleams our Banner...*Ar'd.*	26
Calm..................*Handel Pond*	124
Children's Voices.............*Arranged*	99
Child's Desire ....*Anon.*	25
Christ Hath Arisen................ *	20
Christmas Carol...*Rev. E. P. Parker*	17
Christmas Song...*Rev. E. P. Parker*	18
Come Jesus Redeemer............ *	59
Come let us Sing of Jesus...*Arranged*	24
Come, little Children, Come....*Arr'd*	40
Come Sing with Gladness, *W. B. Bradbury*	55
Come to Me.........*Rev. E. P. Parker*	106
Come, ye Faithful...............*Anon.*	63
Crusader's Hymn................*Anon.*	73
Dawn..............*Rev. E. P. Parker*	116
Dear Jesus........................	133

	PAGE
Evening Prayer................*Anon.*	102
Fast Fades the Day.............. *	47
Federal Street............*H. K. Oliver*	125
Flee as a Bird......*Rev. E. P. Parker*	64
Gentle Call....................*Arranged*	56
Gentle Shepherd............*Arranged*	66
German Tune ....*Arranged*	48
Glory to Jesus .... *	87
Good Night till Then............ *	72
Good Tidings.......*Rev. E. P. Parker*	23
Great Shepherd of the Sheep *	94
Guide Us and Guard Us....*Arranged*	92
Happy Band of Pilgrims................	33
Hark the Songs of Zion....... *	29
He Leadeth Me......................	54
Holy Saviour, Pray for Me.............	22
Home Above......................	67
Home of the Blest...*Rev. E. P. Parker*	100
Home of the Soul...*Rev. E. P. Parker*	79
Home Returning...*Rev. E. P. Parker*	44
How Loving is Jesus......... *	41
I Love to Hear the Story...*G. F. Root*	65
I Need Thee................*D. F. Hodges*	93
I will give you Rest..*Rev. E. P. Parker*	86
Intercession....................*English*	36
Invitation............*From Wallace*	122
Jerusalem ....*Anon.*	81

INDEX OF TUNES.

	PAGE
Jerusalem the Golden...*Alex. Ewing*	90
Jesus, Holy Saviour.*Rev.E.P.Parker*	107
Jesus is our Shepherd......................	96
Jesus, Lover of my Soul.......*Herold*	115
Jesus, Lord of Life and Glory..*Arr'd*	75
Jesus Most Holy...*Rev. E. P. Parker*	46
Jesus, still Lead on.............*A. Drese*	66
Jesus, Tender Saviour .... *	37
Jesus waiting to Enter............*Anon.*	77
Keble............................... *German*	120
Lead them to Thee ...*Rev. R. Lowry*	108
Lent................................... *	53
Light from Heaven..........*Arranged*	69
Manoah..................................	126
My Heart is Resting............. *	51
My Saviour Dear...................*Anon.*	91
O Paradise.......................... *	84
O'er the Silent River, *Rev. E. P. Parker*	28
One by One.........*Rev. E. P. Parker*	42
Onward, Christian Soldiers, *From Haydn*	80
Our Loving Redeemer.*W.B.Bradbury*	30
Our Song of Triumph, *Rev. Alfred Taylor*	39
Pleasant Pastures......*Geo. F. Ryder*	43
Rejoice, Rejoice, Believers.... *	74
Rest............................*Anon.*	132
Resurrection Hymn..............*Haydn*	21
Riverside............*Rev. E. P. Parker*	78
Roll On..............*Rev. E. P. Parker*	88

	PAGE
Saviour, Lead Us................*Haydn*	71
Shepherd-Call......................*Anon.*	40
Song to the Saviour............. *	50
South Church......*Rev. E. P. Parker*	128
Spanish Hymn ....*Anon.*	101
Stand up for Jesus..*Rev. E. P. Parker*	97
Still Chanting as ye Go, *Rev. E. P. Parker*	61
Stockwell ....*Rev. D. E. Jones*	118
Strangers and Pilgrims, *L. O. Emerson*	111
The Best Friend..............*Arranged*	85
The Better World................ *	49
The Children's Hymn........... *	34
The Holy Angels................. *	58
The Jasper Sea............ *W. H. Doane*	76
The Love of Jesus...*Rev. E. P. Parker*	68
The Name of Jesus......................	95
The Other Side...........*J. E. Gould*	52
The Prayer of Devotion....*Arranged*	83
The Saviour's Call.................*Anon.*	60
The Saviour's Legacy, *Rev. J. B. Dykes*	114
The Sunday School Army, *Rev. E. P. Parker*	112
The Voice of Jesus........*From Spohr*	57
The Voice of the Saviour...... *	45
There is a Green Hill........... *	70
Thy Will be Done........................	32
Vienna..............................*Haydn*	35
Watch and Pray...*Rev. E. P. Parker*	27
Wanderer, do not Tarry.. *W.H.Doane*	89
Zion, City of God, *Partly from Kücken*	103

INDEX OF FIRST LINES.

	PAGE
All glory, laud and honor	87
All hail the power of	86
All my heart this night rejoices	23
Alleluia, alleluia	21
Always with us, always with us	118
Art thou weary, art thou.	60
As down in the sunless retreats	83
Beautiful Sion, the home of the soul	79
Blessed Jesus, gracious Saviour	48
Blessed Saviour thee I love	101
Blest are the sons of peace	117
Brightest and best of the sons	19
Brightly gleams our banner	26
Calm on the listening ear	18
Children's voices high in heaven	99
Christ hath arisen.	20
Christian, seek not yet repose	27
Come, Holy Spirit, come.	117
Come Holy Spirit, heavenly	123
Come, Jesus Redeemer, abide	59
Come, kingdom of our God.	131
Come, let us sing of Jesus	24
Come, little children, come.	40
Come sing with holy gladness	55
Come, sinner to the gospel feast	122
Come, thou fount of every	128
Come to me, come to me	106
Come unto me cried the voice	45
Come unto me when shadows	86
Come, wandering sheep.	40
Creator, Preserver, Redeemer	50
Dear Jesus, e'er at my side	133
Fairest Lord Jesus	73
Father, whate'er of earthly	127
Flee as a bird to your	64

	PAGE
For all thy saints O God.	124
Gathering homeward from every land	42
Gentle Shepherd grant thy	66
Gently, Lord, O gently lead us	118
Glorious things of thee are spoken	103
God rest ye all good people	17
Gracious Spirit, love divine	119
Great Shepherd of the sheep	94
Hark, hark, my soul, angelic	104
Hark the songs of peaceful Zion	29
He leadeth me, oh, blessed	54
Heavenly Father, send thy	35
How could I know the way	110
How gentle God's commands	131
How loving is Jesus who came.	41
How sweet to be allowed to pray	126
How sweet to leave the world	121
I heard the voice of Jesus say	57
I journey forth rejoicing	72
I lay my sins on Jesus	82
I love the holy angels	58
I love thy kingdom, Lord	117
I love to hear the story	65
I love to steal awhile away	122
I need thee, precious Jesus	93
I think when I read that sweet	25
If thy days are full of sorrow	89
In the cross of Christ I glory	119
Jerusalem so bright and fair	62
Jerusalem the golden	90
Jesus, lover of my soul	115
Jesus, still lead on	66
Jesus, tender Saviour	37
Jesus, tender Shepherd, hear	102
Just as I am, without	121

INDEX OF FIRST LINES.

	PAGE
Lead them, my God, to thee	108
Light of those whose dreary	129
Lord, I hear that showers of	128
Lord, in this thy mercy's day	53
March along, march along	39
My faith looks up to thee	129
My God, my Father, while	32
My heart is resting, O my God	51
My Jesus, as thou wilt	132
My Saviour bids me come	130
My Saviour dear, my Saviour	91
My Saviour stands waiting and	98
My spirit on thy care	124
Nearer, my God, to thee	113
Not all the blood of beasts	117
O cease, my wandering soul	116
O for a closer walk with God	123
O happy band of pilgrims	33
O holy Saviour, pray for me	22
O how my spirit longs for	67
O Jesus, thou art standing	77
O love divine that stooped	125
O mother dear, Jerusalem	81
O my Saviour, Guardian true	119
O Paradise, O Paradise	84
O watch and pray, fast fades	47
O what a lovely path	123
O what, if we are Christ's	131
O when shall I dwell in a	100
One sweetly solemn thought	116
One there is above all	85
Onward, Christian soldiers	80
Our blest Redeemer, ere he	114
Our life is but a fading	114
Our loving Redeemer we trust	30
Pleasant are the pastures where	43

	PAGE
Rejoice, rejoice, believers	74
Rejoice, ye pure in heart	61
Rock of ages, cleft for me	129
Saviour and Lord of all	92
Saviour, like a shepherd lead	71
Shall we gather at the river	109
Sing to the Lord the children's	34
Soon will our weeping time	88
Sun of my soul, thou Saviour	120
Stand up, stand up for Jesus	97
Take my heart, O Father	119
The Comforter has come	130
The roseate hues of early	127
The Spirit in our hearts	131
The Sunday School army has	112
There is a better world they say	49
There is a blessed home	132
There is a fountain filled	127
There is a green hill far away	70
There is an hour of hallowed	127
There is no love like the love	68
There's a friend for little	38
This life so brief is full of	111
Thou dear Redeemer, dying	123
To-day the Saviour calls	60
To whom, my Saviour, can I	126
We are waiting by the river	78
We dwell this side of Jordan's	52
When for me the silent oar	28
When I survey the wondrous	120
When the weary seeking rest	36
When we've crossed the jasper	76
While on life's stormy sea	69
With tearful eyes I look	121
Worthy the Lamb of boundless	121
Yes, kind Saviour, grieving	44

THE
BOOK OF PRAISE:
OR,
Hymns and Tunes
FOR
PUBLIC AND SOCIAL WORSHIP,

PREPARED UNDER THE SANCTION AND AUTHORITY, AND IN BEHALF OF THE GENERAL ASSOCIATION.

FOURTEENTH EDITION.

The Book of Praise is offered to the churches in eight styles with music, and six without.

This work is now so largely introduced, and the Publishers have received so many commendatory notices from eminent clergymen and musical leaders, that they feel warranted in recommending it to the favorable consideration of churches.

Copies *for examination* will be sent, post-paid, by mail to Pastors and Committees on receipt of one dollar.

Address
HAMERSLEY & CO.,
HARTFORD, CONN.

"THE MOST ENGAGING AND DESIRABLE COLLECTION OF ITS KIND."

SONG FLOWERS

FOR THE

Sunday=School and Social Meeting.

Eleventh Edition; Revised and Enlarged.

BY

Rev. E. P. PARKER.

The attention of Pastors and of Superintendents of Sunday-Schools is called to this collection. It was prepared with the express purpose of giving to the Sunday-School, hymns of a devotional character, and music of a substantial, and at the same time, popular nature.

The first edition, though it was not advertised, was immediately bought up, and a new edition was urgently called for. The new edition has been enriched by fifty new tunes and a large number of very choice hymns, and is well adapted for use in the social prayer meeting. From many quarters the author has received the most grateful acknowledgments of the value of his work.

PUBLISHED BY . HAMERSLEY & CO.,
263 Main Street, Hartford, Conn.

Price, 35 Cents a copy, bound in boards; to Sunday-Schools, $30 per hundred, cash.

SUNDAY SCHOOL SONGS:
A NEW COLLECTION OF HYMNS AND TUNES,
SPECIALLY PREPARED FOR THE USE OF SUNDAY SCHOOLS AND FOR SOCIAL AND FAMILY WORSHIP.

By REV. E. P. PARKER—Third Edition.

"Rev. E. P. Parker, of Hartford, edits, and edits *well*, Sunday School Songs."—[*The Advance*, Dec. 16, 1869.

" The Sunday School Songs differs from most of the books of the present day, being made up entirely of Christian hymns. We are glad to see it, and hope it may find its way into very many of our Sunday Schools."—[*Christian Mirror*, December 14, 1869.

The *Christian Secretary* styles the Rev. Mr. Parker's SUNDAY SCHOOL SONGS " a gem among the music books."

"SUNDAY SCHOOL SONGS, by Rev. E. P. Parker, commends itself to us as especially meritorious, in that its selections of music have a much higher range than usual, avoiding the fault remarked upon above, while sufficiently popular and diversified in its style to be pleasing to all."—[*The Congregationalist*, Dec., 1869.

" SUNDAY SCHOOL SONGS" is a new collection of hymns and tunes, specially prepared for the use of Sunday Schools and for family and social worship, by Rev. E. P. Parker, published in Hartford by Hamersley & Co. This small book contains but very little of the ordinary balderdash, either in words or music, and a very large proportion of really excellent hymns, pleasant chords, and sweet melodies. Both in words and music, these songs are infinitely superior to the trash in common use throughout our country. If musical composers and publishers generally would exercise the literary taste which Mr. Parker has shown in the books of sacred song to which he has given their character, the happy day for which we sigh would soon dawn, when Sunday School singing will cease to be a disgrace to our churches and an insult to the Deity. In the present volume, Mr. Parker has rejected weak choruses and repetitions more rigidly than in 'Song Flowers.' That he may continue to grow in this grace of a happy literary conservatism, is our heartfelt prayer."—[*The Independent*, January 13, 1870.

We are constantly receiving from the press, from clergymen, and from Sunday-school superintendents, flattering notices of this book.

We also continue to publish the "SONG FLOWERS," by the same author, some ten editions of which have been printed and sold. The music and hymns of these two books is decidedly better than the great majority of Sabbath-school song books.

The price of the two books is the same; namely, 35 cents per copy singly —$30 per hundred, CASH. Copies sent to any address, prepaid, on receipt of 35 cents.

HAMERSLEY & CO., Publishers, Hartford, Conn.

VALUABLE SCHOOL BOOKS

PUBLISHED BY

HAMERSLEY & CO.,

HARTFORD, CONN.,

And to be obtained through the principal Booksellers of the Country.

SWIFT'S FIRST LESSONS ON NATURAL PHILOSOPHY. Part First and Second, making two Books. Revised and enlarged editions, with numerous illustrations, containing new chapters on electricity, the daguerreotype, &c.

The remarkable success of the first editions of these two books has abundantly proved that natural science can be made clear to the minds of young children, and that these books are eminently adapted to that purpose, having gained for themselves a circulation in every State in the Union. Their great success has induced the publishers to bring out an enlarged edition. For simplicity of style and aptness of illustration, Miss Mary A. Swift has obtained a reputation as wide as our country.

ROBBINS' OUTLINES OF ANCIENT AND MODERN HISTORY: on a new plan. Embracing Biographical Notices of Illustrious Persons, and General Views of the Geography, Population, &c., &c., of Ancient and Modern Nations. With Questions. New and revised edition.

The great number of editions that have been called for, furnish ample evidence of its merits. It is a clear and concise compend, from the hands of an accomplished writer, and is arranged with such taste and judgment as to make it a very attractive work, both to teacher and scholar. It is used with great acceptance throughout the country, and such is its entire impartiality that no charge has, to the knowledge of the publishers, ever been made against the book as exhibiting any undue bias, or deviating from the strictest fairness. Being thus attractive in style, clear, concise, methodically arranged, accurate and impartial, the publishers confidently ask for it an attentive examination.

We desire all teachers not acquainted with this work to examine it, and as an inducement we will send it prepaid by mail, to any teacher who wishes to examine with a view of introducing it in the school they are connected with, on receipt of one dollar.

GALLAUDET'S AND HOOKER'S PRACTICAL SPELLING-BOOK: with Reading Lessons. This Spelling-Book is extensively used, and has received the most decided commendation from practical teachers and other friends of education. As it is on a new plan, it must be examined to be properly appreciated.

ADVERTISEMENTS.

CLASS-BOOK OF NATURE. Comprising Lessons on the Universe — the Three Kingdoms of Nature, and the Form and Structure of the Human Body, &c., with Questions and numerous Engravings. Improved edition.

GREEK SERIES.

The following series of Greek text-books has been received with great favor by classical teachers. Sophocles' Greek Grammar is used in Harvard, and many other colleges of the Union, and in a large number of high schools and academies. The text-books prepared by President Woolsey of Yale College, are too well known to classical teachers to need any comment.

FIRST BOOK IN GREEK. By *E. A. Sophocles*, Professor of Greek in Harvard University, Cambridge.

GREEK LESSONS. Adapted to the revised edition of the author's Greek Grammar for the use of beginners. By *E. A. Sophocles*.

GREEK GRAMMAR, first edition. For the use of Schools and Colleges. By *E. A. Sophocles*.

GREEK GRAMMAR, new edition. For the use of Schools and Colleges. By *E. A. Sophocles*.

GREEK EXERCISES. For Schools and Colleges. By *E. A. Sophocles*.

ROMAIC GREEK GRAMMAR. By *E. A. Sophocles*.

A GREEK READER, for the use of Schools. Containing selections in Prose and Poetry, with English Notes and a Lexicon. By *C. C. Felton* President of Harvard College.

ELEMENTS OF GREEK GRAMMAR. By *Chauncey A. Goodrich*. Heretofore published as the Grammar of *Casper Frederic Hachenburg*.

THE GORGIAS OF PLATO, with Notes. By *Theodore D. Woolsey*, LL. D., President of Yale College. Revised edition of 1870.

THE ANTIGONE OF SOPHOCLES, with Notes. By *Theodore D. Woolsey*, LL. D., President of Yale College. Revised edition of 1870.

THE ALCESTIS OF EURIPIDES, with Notes. By *Theodore D. Woolsey*, LL. D., President of Yale College. Revised edition of 1870.

THE ELECTRA OF SOPHOCLES, with Notes. By *Theodore D. Woolsey*, LL. D., President of Yale College. Revised edition of 1870.

THE PROMETHEUS OF ÆSCHYLUS, with Notes. By *Theodore D. Woolsey*, LL. D., President of Yale College. Revised edition of 1870.

THE BOOK OF PRAISE.

THE BOOK OF PRAISE, or Hymns and Tunes for Public and Social Worship, prepared under the sanction and authority, and in behalf of the General Association. 8vo. 406 pages. Recommended by two hundred clergymen, eminent laymen, and the religious Press.

Leather back, cloth sides, Full Sheep raised bands, French Morocco marbled edge, French Morocco gilt edge, Turkey extra gilt. Cheaper edition, with type as large as the above, Full Cloth, Full Sheep, French Morocco.

ADVERTISEMENTS.

THE BOOK OF PRAISE, or Hymns (only) for Public and Social Worship, prepared under the sanction and authority, and in behalf of the General Association. 16mo. 672 pages.

Leather back cloth sides, Full Sheep, French Morocco sprinkled edge, French Morocco gilt edge, Turkey extra gilt. Cheaper edition, with type as large as the above, Full Cloth, Full Sheep, French Morocco.

THE SABBATH HYMN AND HYMN AND TUNE BOOK SERIES.

By Edwards A. Park, D.D., Austin Phelps, D.D., and Lowell Mason, Mus. Doc.

THE SABBATH HYMN BOOK. Small quarto edition, Brevier type, double columns, 336 pages, with Index of First Lines of Hymns and Index of Authors, printed on superfine paper. *A very neat and attractive edition.* In binding, Cloth, Full Sheep, Morocco.

Sixteenmo Edition, containing 962 pages, with very large type, including the following Indexes — Classification of Hymns, Alphabetical Index of Subjects, Index of Subjects of Selections for Chanting, Index of Scriptural Passages, Index of First Lines of Hymns, Index of First Lines of Stanzas, and Index of Authors, printed on superfine paper, in various bindings. Sheep, Morocco, Morocco gilt edge, Turkey Antique and gilt, stiff and flexible gilt edge.

THE SABBATH HYMN AND TUNE BOOK, with plain tunes, containing all the Hymns set to appropriate tunes, the words and the music being on the same page.

THE NEW SABBATH HYMN AND TUNE BOOK, with popular tunes, with the same arrangement of Hymns, and the same Indexes, but with different tunes. In place of the Anthems in the other edition are a number of popular tunes. About three hundred and twenty-five thousand people are using this series.

Sixteenmo Edition, Brevier type corresponding with the large edition page for page, except that the Topical Index is omitted. Cloth extra, Morocco, Morocco gilt edges.

Octavo Edition, with large plain type, including a full Topical Index. Cloth extra, Morocco; Morocco gilt edges, Turkey Morocco, in various patterns.

THE SABBATH TUNE BOOK, containing the tunes only. Cloth.

BAPTIST EDITIONS.

Editions of the above, prepared expressly for the use of Baptist Churches, by *Francis Wayland, D.D., LL. D.*, consisting of

THE SABBATH HYMN BOOK, Baptist Edition.

Small Quarto Edition. Cloth, Sheep, Morocco. Sixteenmo Edition. Sheep, Morocco, Morocco gilt edges, Turkey Morocco, gilt edges, plain, or flexible, or full gilt.

www.ingramcontent.com/pod-product-compliance
Lightning Source LLC
Chambersburg PA
CBHW020053170426
43199CB00009B/273